Frank Hamilton Taylor

From the St. Johns to the Apalachicola

Or, Through the Uplands of Florida

Frank Hamilton Taylor

From the St. Johns to the Apalachicola
Or, Through the Uplands of Florida

ISBN/EAN: 9783744757096

Printed in Europe, USA, Canada, Australia, Japan

Cover: Foto ©Andreas Hilbeck / pixelio.de

More available books at **www.hansebooks.com**

THE
CHILDREN'S PREACHER

THE
CHILDREN'S PREACHER

A YEAR'S ADDRESSES AND PARABLES
FOR THE YOUNG.

BY

REV. J. REID HOWATT,

AUTHOR OF

"THE CHURCHETTE," "THE CHILDREN'S PULPIT," "THE CHILDREN'S
PEW," "THE CHILDREN'S PRAYER BOOK," "AFTER HOURS,"
"LIFE WITH A PURPOSE," ETC., ETC.

New York:
THOMAS WHITTAKER,
2 AND 3 BIBLE HOUSE.
1897.

To

W. P. TRELOAR, Esq.,

"THE CHILDREN'S ALDERMAN,"

With many a friendly memory of old times and new,
I respectfully dedicate
this other book for the bairns.

PREFACE

TEN years ago I ventured, with diffidence, to lay the foundation of a children's cathedral, by "The Churchette." The encouragement given to this led to its being followed by "The Children's Angel," as a kind of guardian. "The Children's Pulpit" was next reared, and afterwards "The Children's Pew;" so that with the present volume, "The Children's Preacher," all the requirements for a Children's Sanctuary are fairly met, if He, without Whose presence there can be no Church, will graciously vouchsafe to let the light of His glory fall upon all. Again, too, I have to express my deep indebtedness for permission to reproduce what originally appeared in *The Home Messenger*, *Sunday Magazine*, *The New Age*, and other periodicals.

How the work of ministering to the young has advanced in these ten years! It is only twice that term since "a word to the children" came to be seriously regarded as a part of the weekly service, but they were few who then regularly availed themselves of the opportunity. If now, however, there are any who, while feeding the sheep, feel that the lambs are beyond them, no one mourns the circumstance more than they do themselves. Many of these are the very best of men, with biggest love for bairns in their hearts, but some early failures in speaking to the children have made them shy of attempting the work again. I have cause to sympathise with all such, and to help them if I can. I shiver still at the recollection of my first attempts; they were dictatorial, if not pragmatic, with the suggestion of chalk and a blackboard being somewhere on the premises; or else they were simply silly! I believe I would have abandoned this part of my work altogether but for the help I got from two simple rules. One was—*See all things from a child's height.* He sees the under side of the leaves where you see the upper; what is to you but a hole in a bank is to him a cave. This has been one of the best helps I have had, both for understanding children and for keeping the child alive in my own breast. The other rule was—*Resolutely ignore the presence of the old folk when you are dealing with children.* See, think of, feel that young ones, and young ones only, are round you, and you will smile, be at ease, and hold the children, as you know very well how to do when you have gathered two or three about your knee. For the rest, be less particular about the words you use than about the impression you are making. Children are not stylists, but they are quick to catch the drift of your meaning even though this word or that should, of itself, be out of their depth. Let any one sail out on this tack for a month or two, and he will find the joy of the most pleasing part of our ministry.

That this may help all who seek to help the little ones to the Good Shepherd, and that by it many young ones may be led to the Lord and be directed on the daily way, is my humble prayer.

J. R. H.

CAMBERWELL, *June* 18, 1896.

CONTENTS

I
THE WISE KNIGHT .   PAGE 1

II
THE TENT, THE ALTAR, AND THE WELL .   4
> "And he builded an altar there, and called upon the name of the Lord, and pitched his tent there: and there Isaac's servants digged a well."—GEN. xxvi. 25.

III
BETWIXT AND BETWEEN .   9
> "He was more honourable than the thirty, but he attained not to the first three."—2 SAM. xxiii. 23.

IV
A STIRRING STORY .   14
> "Christ died for us."—ROM. v. 8.

V
THE SWORD OF LOVE .   16
> "My sword shall be bathed in heaven."—ISA. xxxiv. 5.

VI
A TOUGH FIGHT .   20
> "He went down and slew a lion in a pit in a snowy day."—1 CHRON. xi. 22.

VII

THE AMBULANCE CORPS . . . 24

"A young man of Egypt."—1 SAM. xxx. 13.

VIII

THE FERRY BOAT 29

"And there went over a ferry boat to carry over the king's household, and to do what he thought good."—2 SAM. xix. 18.

IX

HEAVEN'S GATE 32

"This is the gate of heaven."—GEN. xxviii. 17.

X

OUR PROPER PLACE 36

"It shall be given to them for whom it is prepared."—MARK x. 40.

XI

OUR HOME ABROAD 40

XII

BREAKING THE SPELL 42

"The great trumpet shall be blown."—ISA. xxvii. 13.

XIII

CHILD-VISION 47

"Thou hast hid these things from the wise and prudent, and hast revealed them unto babes."—MATT. xi. 25.

XIV

CLEAR THE LINE! . . . 51

"Seek ye first."—MATT. vi. 33.

XV

AGAINST THE STREAM 57

"So did *not* I, because of the fear of the Lord."—NEH. v. 15.

XVI

IN THEIR RIGHT ORDER 61

"The child Samuel ministered unto the Lord before Eli."—1 SAM. iii. 1.

XVII

SO TIRED! 65

"Jesus, being wearied with His journey, sat thus on the well."—JOHN iv. 6.

XVIII

THE WINDING WAY 69

"They went up with winding stairs."—1 KINGS vi. 8.

XIX

HOPING AND WAITING 75

"It is good that a man should both hope and quietly wait for the salvation of the Lord."—LAM. iii. 26.

XX

THE MAGIC CRYSTAL 80

"Now we see through a glass, darkly; but then face to face."—1 COR. xiii. 12.

XXI

SPRING-TIME 84

"The flowers appear on the earth."—SONG OF SOL. ii. 12.

XXII

SOWING AND REAPING 88

"A sower went forth to sow."—MATT. xiii. 3.

XXIII

YOU AND I AND EVERYBODY 90

"A wise man's heart is at his right hand: but a fool's heart at his left."—ECCLES. x. 2.

XXIV

GIVING AND GETTING 94

"All things come of Thee, and of Thine own have we given Thee."—1 CHRON. xxix. 14.

XXV

LAMP AND OIL 96

"They that were foolish took their lamps, and took no oil with them. But the wise took oil in their vessels with their lamps."—MATT. xxv. 3, 4.

XXVI

A QUESTION OF TASTE 101

"Is there any taste in the white of an egg?"—JOB vi. 6.

XXVII

A NARROW ESCAPE 107

"Be ye thankful."—COL. iii. 15.

XXVIII

ROOM AND POWER TO LET 110

"I am not ashamed of the gospel of Christ: for it is the power of God unto salvation, to every one that believeth."—ROM. i. 16.

XXIX

A TALK ABOUT TONGUES 119

XXX

ANSWERS TO PRAYERS 123

"And all the devils besought Him, saying, Send us into the swine."
"And they began to pray Him to depart out of their coasts."
"He . . . prayed Him that he might be with Him."—
MARK v. 12, 17, 18.

XXXI

SWEETER THAN HONEY 128

"The law of kindness."—PROV. xxxi. 26.

XXXII

DRY STICKS 137

"Lay my staff upon the face of the child."—2 KINGS iv. 29.

XXXIII

CROWN RIGHTS 141

"As we have, therefore, opportunity, let us do good unto all."—GAL. vi. 10.

XXXIV

"BRAKES DOWN!" 147

"Slow to speak."—JAMES i. 19.

XXXV

BIG-HEARTED 152

"Who is my neighbour?"—LUKE x. 29.

XXXVI

Multum in Parvo 154

"Even a child is known by his doings."—Prov. xx. 11.

XXXVII

Pilot Wanted! 158

"Made shipwreck."—1 Tim. i. 19.

XXXVIII

The Kind Heart 162

"Thou shalt not see thy brother's ox or his sheep go astray, and hide thyself from them: thou shalt in any case bring them again unto thy brother."—Deut. xxii. 1.

XXXIX

Inward Riches 165

"Goodly pearls."—Matt. xiii. 45.

XL

Monkey Tricks 170

"Apes."—1 Kings x. 22.

XLI

Big and Little 175

"Some great thing."—2 Kings v. 13.

XLII

Building 180

"Stone made ready before it was brought thither."—1 Kings vi. 7.

XLIII

NOT TOO PARTICULAR . . . 185

"Where no oxen are, the crib is clean."—PROV. xiv. 4.

XLIV

THE TEMPTER 190

"Again there was a day when the sons of God came to present themselves before the Lord, and Satan came also among them, to present himself before the Lord. And the Lord said unto Satan, From whence comest thou? And Satan answered the Lord, and said, From going to and fro in the earth, and from walking up and down in it."—JOB ii. 1, 2.

XLV

NEAT KNOTS 194

"Sins that are past."—ROM. iii. 25.

XLVI

THE SCENT OF LIFE 197

"In the Spirit."—REV. i. 10.

XLVII

OPEN SECRETS 202

"Dark sayings."—PS. lxxviii. 2.

XLVIII

HOW TO BEGIN THE DAY . . . 207

"It is a good thing to give thanks unto the Lord, and to sing praises unto Thy name, O most High: to show forth Thy lovingkindness in the morning, and Thy faithfulness every night."—PS. xcii. 1, 2.

XLIX

Don't grow Old 209

L

"When He cometh" 213

"They shall be Mine, saith the Lord of hosts, in that day when I make up My jewels."—Mal. iii. 17.

LI

An Improbable Story 217

LII

Dicky Boy 221

"The star, which they saw in the east, went before them, till it came and stood over where the young child was."—Matt. ii. 9.

LIII

A New Start 233

THE CHILDREN'S PREACHER

I

THE WISE KNIGHT

HE was a good and noble King, who loved the right and hated evil. A great sorrow lay on his heart as he looked on many of his subjects and saw how they lived. He had spoken to them, and tried to make them better, but they soon forgot what he said.

"How can I make them to know?" he asked, half to himself, and half to the courtiers who were round him, as he looked from the palace window over the city and the gardens, and the far-stretching plains beyond. "I have given them good laws; I have protected their fields; they have had peace; but how many of them are living for themselves alone, and their eyes never go up to God! How can I make them understand?"

He was lost in reverie, till some movement made him look down; and there, bending low before him, a figure knelt, covered and shrouded with gossamer gauze that floated dark but soft as a cloud about him. He was the Wise Knight, who had come from a foreign land; he loved the King, and was faithful to him, and the King knew him to be good and true.

"Speak," said the King, looking kindly down; and the Knight lifted his face, so dark, but beautiful beyond the power of tongue to tell, and his eyes were like homes of pity.

"By the Shadow, my liege," he said, "by the Shadow."

Then the King bade him stand, and they talked in low tones, looking out on the city and fields at times, and pointing here and there.

Then the Knight from the foreign land drew the filmy cloud of the dark gossamer round him till his face was hidden, and softly glided away.

But the King kept watch from the palace window.

It was a glorious day; the sun was scattering gold everywhere, and the soft breeze was kind. Men and women and little children, with work and play, were making the music to which the world rolls on.

And the Shadow moved among them: the Shadow of a cloud. It moved on and on, and nothing could keep it back. It stepped lightly over the loftiest walls; it went dry-footed through the streams; it walked from top to top of the trees, yet never a leaf bent under its weight.

It fell on a man who had hate in his heart, and bit

by bit the hate passed away, and a strange peace came.

It fell on a woman as the eye of a serpent was fixed upon her, and was drawing her closer and closer ; and in the Shadow the jewelled eye grew dull: she saw the serpent and escaped.

It fell on a man who was gathering stones to add to the height of a great house he was building; and the house seemed strange with the Shadow on it: it looked like a tomb; and the man knelt and prayed a prayer he had forgotten for many a year.

It fell on a poor convict labouring in the field with a chain on his ankles, and he wiped his brow, his face grew beautiful, and he lifted his eyes to God.

So the Shadow passed from field to field, and house to house, and land to land, and wherever it fell there was chill and fear, but when it was gone there came quiet and blessing, and every fountain was made fresher, every flower was made fairer, every soul was made better, for the touch of the Shadow.

Can you read the riddle?

The Knight is Suffering: his King is God: his work is—Love.

II

THE TENT, THE ALTAR, AND THE WELL

> "And he builded an altar there, and called upon the name of the Lord, and pitched his tent there: and there Isaac's servants digged a well."—GEN. xxvi. 25.

THIS is all about Isaac—the kind of man he was, and the kind of thing he did. But it is also all about you, and me, and everybody. How? Well, we must find that out.

If I were asked to draw a picture which would be like a book for showing everybody what he was like, and what he should be, and what he should do, this is the picture I would draw—a tent, an altar, and a well. In these three things, and what they mean, you have everything that is needed to make your life be right, and perfect, and good.

THE TENT.—You know what it is like—a rough thing made of canvas or of skins, which soon gets stained with the weather, and, however dainty it may have been at the first, before very long needs patching here and mending there, and propping up somewhere else.

Would you wish to live in a tent? You don't need

to wish for it; you have got your wish already. You *are* living in a tent now! Yes; your body is only a tent. It is nothing more—nothing! *You* are not your body, any more than the person inside the tent is the tent. You yourself are something very different from the body. Why, the body is always being changed, being worn away, and patched, and mended, so that in a very few months there isn't a single bit left of the body that was there some months before.

But what about you—you yourself—the real boy or the real girl inside this tent? You haven't been rubbed away in that fashion, have you? You can still remember things that happened years ago, and the lessons you learnt when first you went to school you have kept still. The tent, you see, is always being patched and mended, till there isn't a bit of the old canvas left after a time, and then gets patched and mended again and yet again; but you yourself, you remain in the midst of it all, like the one who dwells in the tent but isn't at all a part of the tent himself.

Yes, children, we all dwell in tents, just like Isaac, and the tent is always changing, changing—changing in itself, changing in its place; sometimes it is nearly blown down with sickness, sometimes it is beautiful and comfortable with health, sometimes it is pitched where the grass is green, sometimes it is pitched where there is only a weary wilderness round us; but at last—at last—the tent is broken up and cast down, and we have to come out. And we call that *death*. Death is just the complete casting down of the tent, so that we must step out. After that the journeying is over, the tent is not needed, we shall live without the body. It was only a tent for the soul for a time; it is the soul that is the real boy or girl, man or woman, within the tent.

Then what about that time—when the soul must step out? Where is it to go? It must go somewhere. Which direction shall it take—up or down? to the light and to gladness, or to the darkness and sorrow? Ah! there is no need to ask; we should all want it to turn to the light and the gladness, and have a sweet, kind home with God. Then, if we would find that at the last, it is now—while we are yet in the tent—yet in the body—we must learn the way. It is by—

The Altar.—The altar means prayer, means worship, means praise, means faith—means whatever brings and keeps us near to God. And so Jesus is called our Altar because it is through Him only we can learn about God, and learn how to make sure of the right road when the tent is thrown down at last and we have to step out.

Just think of it! Here we are—a regular encampment—so many tents that are called bodies; and yet inside every one of these there is a soul that is going one day to step out free from the body altogether, and is going to live for ever and ever! It is a curious thing to think about, is it not? Sometimes the Arabs will remain a long time in the same place, dwelling in their tents, but suddenly the tents will all be struck and the people will move swiftly away. But there will be no confusion, no cries, no fears. They know where they are going, and they know the way; they have been learning about that while their tents were still standing; and so, when the word comes, they are ready to depart. They have learnt the way they should take.

Shouldn't we do the same? We should.

"Where's your master gone?" a gentleman asked a negro once.

"Don't know, sah," said the negro; "but he's dead."

"Dead? I didn't know of it. Has he gone to heaven?"

"I don't think so, sah," said the dark servant; "he hadn't made no preparations. When he was going away to Saratoga, or New York, or anywhere else, he was always gettin' things ready beforehand, and gettin' them marked; but I never heard him speak about heaven, or about gettin' ready for going there."

Children, do not you be so foolish. Get ready, and get ready now. Wherever the tent is, set up the altar there too. Wherever you are and whatever you do, keep close touch with Jesus. He alone can teach you, and help you, and make you ready against the time when the tent must be cast down and you must go out.

The tent and the altar, the altar and the tent—let these two always go together.

But what about—

THE WELL?—Dig one somewhere, somehow. You can do it. Every deed of kindness you do, every loving word you speak, everything—everything which helps somebody else to be better, or happier, or brighter—is widening and widening a little fountain of love till it becomes like a well, where thirsty lips and dry, parched hearts can be cheered and helped upon their way. Love never fails; no, never! The tent goes away, the moss may grow over the altar and hide it, but the well—ah! that will go sparkling on and on, and bird and beast, and man and child, will be blessed by it, even when your name is forgotten. Dig a well somewhere, somehow, before your soul steps out of its tent; do something good, something kind, something noble, which shall remain after you have gone.

Here, then, as I said, are the three things that should make a perfect life. The tent—that is for yourselves; the altar—that is for God; the well—that is for those around us, and those who shall come after us. The tent is for now; the altar is for hereafter; the well is for hereafter and now both. Love to God—that is the altar; love to man—that is the well; and no one can ever say he loves God unless he loves man too. So, children, as long as you are in the tent, keep by the altar and dig a well. Yours will then be the perfect life.

III

BETWIXT AND BETWEEN

"He was more honourable than the thirty, but he attained not to the first three."—2 SAM. xxiii. 23.

DAVID had three Bands of brave and valiant soldiers. Three men made up the First Band; they were exceedingly brave; they had done mightier deeds than all the others.

Three men also made up the Second Band; they had done wondrous things—things that make the ears tingle still, only to hear of—but they hadn't done such great things as those in the First Band.

There were thirty men in the Third Band; they were heroes, every one of them, and a host in themselves that could turn the scale in any battle, but they had never done the grand things the Second Band had done, nor the grander things that had been done by the First Band. They were—"positive, *good;*" the Second Band was—"comparative, *better;*" the First Band was —"superlative, *best.*"

Here was Benaiah the son of Jehoiada; he was the first of the three in the Second Band, and so was their captain. Wasn't that a fine position to have?

It all depends—depends on how he looked at it. In one way it was a very grand position, and one to make him very humble and thankful to God for putting him into it. For, when he looked *down*—down on the thirty brave men who were beneath him in rank, down on the army of thousands that were beneath these again —he had cause to feel humble and grateful that such great honour should have been put upon him.

But when he looked *up*—up to the three mighty heroes who were above him, and who stood there far nearer the king—he must have felt his position to be very tantalising. He was so near to the top, and yet wasn't there!

So, you see, it all depends which way he looked, whether he was happy, or whether he was wretched.

It is just the same with us all. We are none of us first, and we are none of us last. There is always somebody above us—richer, wiser, or stronger; but there is always somebody beneath us too—poorer, duller, or weaker. And it all depends on ourselves, as it did with Benaiah, which way we look and *how* we look, whether we keep our hearts glad and bright, or whether we make them sad and sour.

It is good to look down. I know a man who had rheumatism, and had it badly enough, and he croaked and croaked about it continually and to everybody, till one day he went with me the rounds of a hospital; and when he saw the great pain, the sickness, and the suffering of the many, many who were there, the first thing he said to me as we came out, was, "I'll never complain of my rheumatism again; it is nothing to what some have to bear." And he kept his word; he stuck his teeth into the bullet, as it were, and bore his suffering in silence, as many a brave man and woman does. Ah, yes, children, it is good at times to look down. It is a fine cure for the dumps to go and see how much worse it is with others, however bad it may be with ourselves. That chases away the clouds, and brings the grateful sunshine into the heart again.

But it can also be bad for us to look down. We may let it make us proud, and conceited, and vain, and stuck-up. But that is because we forget—forget God and a great deal besides. Why are others worse off than we are? Maybe it is simply because they never had a chance. They hadn't such parents as we had, or such an education given them, or such opportunities of showing what was in them. Be sure of it, there was many a man in the Band of Thirty who would have done as bravely as any of The Three if he had had their chance; and there are many of those we look down upon who would have done better than any of us if only they had had the opportunity. So, shame upon us if we grow proud! shame upon us if we grow vain because we are better than others! That shows we have forgotten God altogether, and forgotten to pity those who have never had our chance, but are just as good in themselves. Learn to look down, then, children, but learn to look down with love in your eyes, and that will always keep gratitude to God and kindness to men in your heart.

But learn to look up too. There are times, to be sure, when it is bad to do that. It is bad when we look on those who are above us, or are better off than we are, only to envy them, and be spiteful, and grudge them their honour because we are not in their place. That is the way to become miserable and make others miserable too. Remember, we can't all be first. Do you know what makes an editor's life wretched? It is trying to get every man's advertisement at the top of the column. He can't do it, and gets haggard and thin with trying! You see—everybody can't be in the First Band; somebody must be in the Second, and a good many more in the Third.

Then never look up to envy, but look up to admire and imitate. If we look down only, we are apt to grow conceited and lazy and satisfied. But when we look up and see what we have not yet attained to, but perhaps may still be able to reach, then we keep at it, we go on striving and learning, and keeping our wits sharp and our hearts big and hopeful. When you think you are very good and don't need to be made any better, it is because you are looking only on the people about you; but when you look up—up to Jesus, and see how good, and pure, and kind, and loving He is, then you begin to feel very small, and that is the first thing to spur you up to be greater and better.

Whatever your position may be, then, learn how to look wisely both up and down. That will help you to do your duty where you are and as you are, and that, at last—in heaven if not on earth—will bring you into the First Band, for they get nearest Christ who do for His sake whatever they can where He has put them.

IV

A STIRRING STORY

"Christ died for us."—Rom. v. 8.

THERE is a fine tale—just such a tale as you like to hear—told of the old days before there was gunpowder, and when war was a simpler thing than it is now. The enemy came swooping down in the darkness and surrounded a lonely garrison, and hoped to shoot them down, or starve them into surrendering. Yet the soldiers in the garrison had friends, strong friends and many of them; only they couldn't tell them the danger they were in, or call for their help, without lighting the cresset fire which hung by its chain high up, where the enemy could see the man who tried to kindle it, and would shoot him down at the first spark he made. But if ever they were to be delivered that signal must be made; the cresset fire must be kindled.

One man at length stepped forth, and said he would fire the beacon. He knew what it meant; ah, yes! he knew; but he was ready, quite ready. He kneeled and prayed, then sprang to his feet, grasped the torch, leapt on the ramparts, and climbed to the beacon, while a shower of arrows came whizzing upon him. But the beacon was fired; its flame shot up like a cry for help, and their friends understood it and marched to the rescue, and drove back the enemy, and delivered the garrison.

But the poor fellow who had kindled the beacon, where was he? Lying asleep in a soldier's grave. He had died to save his comrades.

Was there a soldier of them all who was saved that night who did not love and honour the man who had saved them? No, not one.

And "Christ died for us"—died for you, died for me, died for everybody. Shouldn't we love Him? shouldn't we praise Him? shouldn't we live for Him? Ah, yes, we should!

If they could have brought the dead soldier to life again, wouldn't they have gladly made him their captain? They would; and so we should make Jesus the Captain of our salvation, for He was brought to life again, and lives to bless us. Be brave, be true, be soldier-like, and stand up for the Lord, who "died for us."

V

THE SWORD OF LOVE

"My sword shall be bathed in heaven."—ISA. xxxiv. 5.

You like to hear about swords; there is something so glittering and sharp about them that they almost magnetise us, as the eye of the serpent is said to magnetise small birds. And there are some rare stories about them, too—from the sword Excalibur which King Arthur had, and which was withdrawn at last by the hand that came out of the lake; and the sword of Scanderbeg, which worked wonders with him, but was useless in the hand of any other (as is the way with many gifts and powers in this world); down to the two-handed sword of Sir William Wallace —there are interesting stories about all of these and about many more, but the sword which the text speaks about is the most interesting of them all, for it is the sword of the Lord.

But we do not like to think of the Lord with a sword in His hand; we would rather think of Him with His hand stretched out to heal and help. Yes, and that is the way He loves best Himself; but there are times when He must use the sword, too. There are sins that need to be struck down, evils that need to be slain, and wickednesses that need to be destroyed. So He must use the sword at times, though He would rather peacefully and lovingly sway the sceptre only.

Do you notice, however, what He says about His sword? "It shall be bathed in heaven." This is a strange thing to say, but it has a deep, deep meaning. What is heaven? Is it not the place of pity, of love, and mercy and goodness? Is there any anger there, or harshness, or hatred, or cruelty? There is none. It is love, and love only, that reigns there supreme.

Then what does He mean when He says that His sword shall be bathed in heaven? Just this: that though the things He does may seem to us to be cruel and harsh, yet there is kindness in them after all; the sword that smites is bathed in love, and when love gives a wound it is in order to make us better when the healing comes.

Is not that the way the doctor works? His lancet is very keen, and he has knives that are very sharp, and he sometimes gives great pain as he uses them. But is he unkind? Is he cruel? No man could be kinder, or mean to be more merciful; what he is trying to do, through all the pain he is giving, is to save us from something or other that would pain us far more at last than all the pain he is giving us for a little.

It is so that God has sometimes to give us pain—to

use His sharp and glittering sword; but that sword is bathed in heaven; there is love in it, and it is a loving hand that is using it. Of course there is pain, there must be pain for a while, but the love that goes with God's sword brings its own sweetness and its own healing for the wound.

This is how it is with God, and it should be the same with us. You, too, have a sword—every one of you. It is the tongue. The Psalmist calls it a sharp sword, and so at times it is and must be. So long as wrong things are done and need to be put right, so long as there is wickedness that needs to be destroyed, just so long must the tongue need to be like a sword. Yes; but what kind of a sword?—one that is bathed in unkindness, or one that is bathed in love? The one is a bad tongue, that does evil even when it is speaking against evil; the other is a good tongue, that does good even when it gives pain.

For example: you know a boy who has done something that is very wrong. Well, you may need to speak to him about it, and that is perhaps all right. But how do you speak to him? Do you only point out how wicked he has been, and how much better you are, and say a great many hard things to him? If that is all you do, then it is a bad sword you are using—one that is bathed in cruelty, not in kindness. The good tongue speaks the truth, but speaks it in love; it points out the fault, not for the sake of fault-finding, but for the sake of doing good, of helping one who has gone wrong to get right again and not lose heart. The bad sword never does good; the good sword never does evil; we may speak the truth, yet be sinning while we are speaking, because we are not speaking in love.

Keep your swords bright and pure, children, as God keeps His, by keeping them bathed in love. If there is anything wrong that needs to be spoken about, or pointed out to be destroyed, before doing it, ask: Why am I going to talk about this? Is it to do any good, or is it only because my own heart is wicked? Never, never use that sword—the sword that is bathed in evil; its wounds rankle and spread, and never do good. Let your sword be the sword of a true knight of the Cross, a sword that is bathed in heaven, a tongue that is sheathed within the lips of love.

VI

A TOUGH FIGHT

"He went down and slew a lion in a pit in a snowy day."—
1 CHRON. xi. 22.

THAT is what he did, and it was counted worth the telling. Why? To give courage to other people, of course. That is what all history is for, or should be for—to show us what others have done, that we may be encouraged to do the like if it is good; or show us where and why they failed, that we may learn to avoid the same mistakes. It must have been a stiff fight. The man was cold and the lion was hungry, but the man got warm as the lion got desperate, and there was no escape for either. All retreat was cut off from both: it had to be a fight to the death of one or other. But perhaps that is not so much to be regretted. There are a great many fights we have to make that we would make all the better, perhaps, if it was a clear case of one or other going down, if there was no retreating. We never really know all we can do till we are fairly put to it. As long as we think there is a chance to shirk, we are sure to take it whenever the struggle becomes extra hard. He was a shrewd old general, and knew what he was about, who was in the habit of putting his men where they *had* to fight, and then making them this simple speech: "There's the enemy, lads; if you don't kill them, they'll kill you!" The men understood, and acted accordingly.

This is something of the spirit we must seek after, for we shall need it. There are sundry lions we also have to meet, and must fight to the death, if we fight them at all. There, for instance, is laziness. You know something about that in the snowy day, do you not? Bed-clothes are very heavy in the morning then; can't lift them off! The fire seems like a magnet; draws you to it and holds you there. There is such a risk in going out. "There's a lion without," you say —or something almost as bad—cold and slipperiness and discomfort. Yes; but there is a bigger lion within —within yourself, for laziness is there, and if you don't kill it, it will one day kill you. Begin the fight there; spring up in the morning at the proper time though your teeth are chattering and you have to break the ice in the basin. Do your duty during the day though the snow should be falling as large as a shilling (or eighteenpence! as some one once described it). Your victory there will help you to many a greater victory elsewhere; but if you fail there, you will fail in a hundred other things, simply because you have not learnt to conquer yourself.

But there, again, is your particular sin. Everybody has some sin that stands up bigger than the rest. With some it is untruthfulness, with others it is sulkiness; with some it is disobligingness, and with some it is selfishness. Whatever it is, it is a lion that must be fought; and there is nothing for it but fighting—hard fighting, too. You can't coax a wild lion, and you can't cut its claws with fine promises. It neither asks nor gives any quarter: you must either kill it or it will kill you. Then, when the case is so clear, don't waste your time by trying any wheedling ways of conquering. Make up your mind—and make up your muscles too—that either it must go down or you must. When it comes to that—a fair fight to the death—then there is all hope for you, but never till then.

But be clear, and be very sure, about this also—that things will always seem to be against you. It is always a snowy day when you fairly face these lions; it is never exactly the kind of weather you would think most suitable. There is always some hindrance in the way. Another day always seems a better day. That is the mistake that has given the lions their chance again and again, so that they have slain their thousands who could have slain them if they had only attacked them boldly when they had the opportunity, without waiting to consider what hindrances seemed in the way. The best day for fighting these lions is—to-day. *Now*—when you know where they are, and what they are—this is the most favourable time you ever will find.

Begin to-day. No matter what hindrances may seem

in the way, the Lord is stronger than all, and in His strength you cannot but win. So offer up a prayer: tell the Lord what you want to overcome; then set yourself determinedly in His strength to do the thing you should do, and you, too, will be reckoned among His "worthies," for you will be more than a conqueror through Him Who loves you.

VII

THE AMBULANCE CORPS

"A young man of Egypt."—1 SAM. xxx. 13.

HERE is the story :—

Four hundred soldiers were sweeping along, tramp, tramp, tramp, with very determined steps. The march was a long one—so long and so swift that they had to leave two hundred of their comrades behind them too exhausted to go any farther. But the four hundred pressed on, every man with his teeth set firmly and his heart beating strong. For they were in pursuit of an enemy who had burned their city to the ground, and had carried away their wives and children, their brothers and sisters, as prisoners; and when men are on the march to rescue those they love, there is apt to be a very strange look in their eyes and a very strong feeling in their hearts.

So they sent out their scouts—men who went far ahead of the rest and spread themselves out like a fan, so that they might find out where the enemy was and not let him take them by surprise. As some of these scouts were hurrying over a field they came on one of the enemy who had caught fever, and had evidently dragged himself into a lonely, shaded corner to die. He was almost dead, but not quite: his heart was still beating. Poor, poor fellow! for three days and nights he had lain there, weak with his sickness, faint with hunger and thirst, waiting for death. Can anything be more pitiful than for a strong man suddenly to find himself become so weak that he can do nothing, *nothing*, to help himself, and with never a soul to do him a kindness in the time of his bitterest need? He had served his master, he had fought for him, he had done his work; but now, when he was sick and of no further use, his master had left him to die like a dog. That is what the devil does to every one who serves him: he gives them plenty of promises so long as he can make use of them; but when the evil they have done at his bidding has come back on themselves, he cares nothing about them—they can die. Ah! the devil is a bad, bad master; his wages always burn at last the hand that takes them.

The scouts stood round the dying man. They could see by his complexion, his uniform and his weapons, that he was one of the enemy who had carried away their wives and children, and that made their fingers twitch on the handles of their swords. They were in haste: every moment was precious if they hoped to come up with the enemy and rescue their loved ones out of his grasp. Would they kill this man at once, then, and march on? No! they would not do that: they were angry men, indignant men, sorrowful men—with good cause to be angry and sorry both—but they were brave men, strong men, and brave men never strike a fallen foe. They would carry him gently to their captain, and get their instructions from him as to what they should do. That is a fine thing, the right thing, to do with an enemy when you have him in your power—take him to Jesus: ask what He would have you do with the one who has done you wrong.

David was in haste, the whole army was in haste, but they sounded a halt as soon as the sick man was brought in. Then they moistened his parched lips and gave him water to drink—(it is "Water! water!" the fevered always moan for)—and gave him something to eat, and the poor sinking soul revived. Then he could tell them all about himself. But he could do more: he could give them information about the enemy they were pursuing, what he had done and the road he had taken; he could conduct them straight to the place where they were camping. Was it mean of this man to turn round on his old comrades? I don't think it was; and I *do* hate meanness—the meanness that splits with a friend and then rushes to tell everything the friend has told in confidence, and that does all it can to harm him. That *is* mean. But this man had never been treated as a friend by those he had been among, but only as a slave. He was an Egyptian, and they were Amalekites: he had been treated as a stranger among strangers all along. And then, when they had got out of him all they could get, and he turned sick and couldn't help himself, they heartlessly dropped him on the way and left him to die in a ditch. I don't think he had any particular cause to feel very friendly to them. Do you?

So David's soldiers crossed their spears, spread their coats upon them, and made a litter for the sick man, and pushed forward again, the Egyptian directing them in the way. By nightfall they came on the enemy eating and drinking and dancing—off their guard, thinking everything was secure. Like angry lions David and his men dashed upon them, slew the most of them, sent the rest flying away in fear, and recovered all who had been taken captive—their wives and little ones—and all the spoil of the Amalekites besides. It was a big victory.

But how did they get it? Wasn't it by showing kindness to one who had been forsaken? Believe it, children, believe it, kindness is never lost. There are poor neglected souls all round you, souls that have long been serving Satan, and found him to be a hard, hard master. Show them kindness; do what you can to bring them to Jesus: as sure as you live you will get a blessing by it and be led to some victory through it. If David and his men had neglected this poor foreigner in his time of need, they would have saved their time perhaps, and a little food and a little trouble, but they would have lost their loved ones. People do lose their loved ones so: they care nothing for the neglected souls around them, and as these increase and grow up, they corrupt and make sinful those they love—and they lose them. God put this weak one in the way of these men; according as they did for him what they should have done, or did not do it, so they would win or lose. Never trouble yourself to ask, then, "Who is my neighbour?" "Who is my friend?" or "Who is my enemy?" Ask, rather, "Who needs me?" "Whom can I help? What can I do to bring some soul to Christ, at home or abroad, and so save it from perishing?" The one you help and have pity upon is the one who in one way or other will lead you to victory; but the one you neglect when you have the chance to do him good but do it not—that one will bring some defeat and disaster upon you. It was the one they had cared nothing for who destroyed the Amalekites at last. Be kind, be kind always; try to be kind to all; the blessing of Jesus lies that way.

VIII

THE FERRY BOAT

"And there went over a ferry boat to carry over the king's household, and to do what he thought good."—2 SAM. xix. 18.

IF you had seen David that night in his tent, you mightn't have thought very much of him. He was just like other people; nothing different. He had no crown on his head or glittering jewels on his garments; his clothes were poor and shabby, and he looked very worn and spent.

Yes; but he was a king, a king every inch of him. For a great promise had been given to him, and it was God who had given it—the promise that he would yet be seated on the throne in Jerusalem, and would have the crown on his head and the sceptre in his hand. Ah! it's a big mistake to judge by appearances. There are people now all round us just like David; they have a hard time of it, and they are sometimes very tired, and they look like very common folk, but yet in the midst of it all they smile, and there is a strange, sweet song always singing in their hearts. It is the song of the promise—God's promise—that they who love the dear Lord Jesus shall yet be kings, and shall reign with Him. They are kings and queens now, though you can see no crown on their brows, for God has said it, and they believe His word—and that is enough—they shall come to the throne yet, for all that they seem so poor. Isn't that worth living for, children? and worth looking for, and striving after? It is—and it can be for you, as it can be for every one; for it is the promise of God to all who believe in the Lord Jesus Christ, and live in the love of Him. Make it your own; take the promise for your very own self. Fix your heart, once and for ever, sure and certain on Jesus Christ, and you shall sit on a throne yet, and wear the crown.

But one thing troubled David that night, as the like has troubled many since. He could not be king till he came to Jerusalem, and there was the river between! The Jordan was broad, and deep, and strong; how would he ever get across? I have known many people troubled about that—very troubled indeed—so long as they were high up on the bank, or far away from the dark, rushing river; but when they came at last down to the brink, there was no difficulty whatever. That was what David found. When he went down in the dark to think it all out, and find if there was any place better than another, he heard a voice speak in the darkness and bid him come, and trust; and there was a boat by the water's edge! And a word was whispered in his ear, and he was no longer afraid, but stepped boldly in, and the boat silently glided away through the gloom. Where he was going he could not tell, but he had the promise, and trusted to it, and was not afraid; and it all turned out as the Lord had promised him: there was a shore beyond, and when he landed on it there were throngs on throngs of friends waiting for him, to accompany him up to the city of palaces and bring him to the kingly throne. The promise was fulfilled: David sat on the throne, and wore the crown and the jewelled robes, and was every way a king.

Trust to God's promise, and live for Jesus, and you need never be afraid of the time when you have to step down to the river. The boat will be ready waiting for you when that hour comes. The boat is black, and the oars dip silently, and the ferryman's face is hidden till you have got across and the sun has risen; then, behold! it is Jesus Christ Himself who has brought you over. That is enough: to be with Him is to be safe. The crown and the throne are certain when Jesus Himself leads us to them.

So live for Him, and live in the trust and hope of the land that lies beyond the river, for Jesus has said, "When thou passest through the waters I will be with thee."

Do you not quite understand all that I mean? Never mind!—only keep it in mind: when you are at the river you will understand, and nobody ever does really understand till then. So trust the promise, and work in love, and—leave the rest with God.

IX

HEAVEN'S GATE

"This is the gate of heaven."—GEN. xxviii. 17.

DID you ever try to run away from your shadow? 'Twas no use. Even when you were sly, and stood quite still and mute as a mouse, and then suddenly bounded away, you couldn't surprise it; it was ready for you and clung still to your very heels. You couldn't shake it off.

Have you ever followed a sunbeam? I have. I remember one cloudy day, when I was going through a great wood where the trees were bare (for it was in the late autumn), and the path was rutty, a sunbeam shone straight down, like a pillar of gold, from a little opening in the clouds, and slowly moved along with me on the way. I wish you had seen me then, clothed in gold, while all round was gloomy! You would have quite thought I was somebody!

Well, it was between the shadow and the sunbeam Jacob lay down to sleep. His shadow was his sin. He had done wrong, and had to run away from home because of it. But he couldn't run away from his shadow; it kept following him all the way, dogging his steps at every turn. He was afraid of God; he thought if he could only get far enough away from the home where God was worshipped he would get beyond God's reach altogether. Many have thought and tried the same, but it has been all in vain.

'Twas a long tramp, and he was tired, very tired, when the night came on and he found himself alone in the wild, rocky wilderness. He wasn't afraid, he was rather glad; for now, he thought, he had got away from his shadow, and right away from God too. So he lay down without a prayer; for what was the use of praying to a God who was far away? But he couldn't help thinking, thinking, as he looked through his half-closing eyes on the great strong stars blazing above him, and on the ledges of rock rising up, tier upon tier, step upon step, in front of him, till they seemed to fade away and come back, and fade again and return, always shining brighter and clearer, and growing more beautiful and more wonderful, till the stars became like the lamps of God, and the rocks became like a silver stairway leading up and up to God's own throne! And the stairway was thronged with angels going and coming on noiseless steps, busy, all of them busy, but busy in such a hush and stillness! And God spoke to Jacob there. He had lain down to sleep at the very gate of heaven!

When he woke in the morning the shadow had gone from his heart. The sunbeam had taken its place, and that sunbeam kept with him all his days to the very last.

Do *you* want to know, then, where heaven is? I can tell you. There is a gate to it, wide open with welcome, close beside the heart of every one who has done wrong and wants to do right, who has sinned and wants to be saved. It doesn't matter where that boy or that girl is—in church or chapel, a little attic or a great cathedral, in the street or in school, among millions of people in a great city, or alone in a wilderness, or in a little boat on the loneliest sea. God is everywhere, and there is a gate to heaven close beside every one who wants to get to heaven. And God is pitiful. Jacob was naughty, but God was kind. Jacob was afraid when he found how close God was. But it wasn't God who made him afraid; it was his old sin. It frightened him to think that God had seen his black shadow. And God *had* seen it, but God was pitiful; He put sunshine into the poor wanderer's heart. Never, never be afraid to go to God. The worse you are and the bigger your sin is, the more He is wishing to help and save you. Pray to Him, then. A penitent prayer never loses its way; it always finds and darts through the gate to heaven.

And trust God to help you when you want to do better, as Jacob wanted now. His strong angels are everywhere, going and coming on errands of mercy. While they have charge of you nothing can hurt you, and Jesus—our Jesus—is Lord of them all.

I don't know where I am going to die, but I know this—wherever I shall lay me down to sleep at last, there—there—will be a gate to heaven. For all places are places of God's dominion. His kingdom is everywhere. He was King of the land Jacob had left, He was King of the land he was sleeping upon, and He was King of the land he was going to. Wherever the pilgrim went, there God was King. Then there is no place where we cannot get help from Him, as Jacob got it; there is no place from which a prayer cannot be sent straight to Him; there is no temptation where His angels cannot protect us; there is no place where we may live or where we may die but close beside it is a gate to heaven. Only love Him with the love that seeks and welcomes Him everywhere—as loving children seek and welcome a loving father—and you will never fail to find Him, and find Him strong to bless.

X

OUR PROPER PLACE

"It shall be given to them for whom it is prepared."
—MARK x. 40.

THERE are some things we can do that God cannot. Think of that! It is quite true, however—and more's the pity. We can do wrong things, for instance, and God cannot; we can do wicked things, but God cannot. We can also do this—we can give honours to people who don't deserve them, and we can keep them back from people who should have them; but God cannot do anything like that. Because He is good, and true, and faithful, He can only make ready for us as we make ready for Him. The place He prepares for every one of us depends on how we have prepared ourselves for the place.

I was once taken over the Observatory at Kew, where wise and learned men study the stars, and get to know what kind of weather we are going to have to-morrow and the day after. I saw such a lot of things there which made me think, and find out my ignorance!

In one room was a great number of watches. I did not expect to find these there—and very cheap watches they seemed to be, with only poor tin or brass cases on them. I asked my friend, the chief of the Observatory, about them, and he explained. These watches, he said, came to him from first-class jewellers in the City, but they were often made by humble workmen in back streets and poor quarters. Some of them were excellent workmen, but no one knew exactly how his work would go until it was tested, so he put it into a cheap case and took it to the jeweller who bought it from him, and he then sent it to the Observatory to be tested.

The testing took a long time. The watch would be left for days and days in a room as hot as the heart of Africa at midsummer, and it would be regulated to stand that heat. Then it would be taken and left for days and days in a room as cold as Greenland in the depths of winter, and it would be watched and regulated again to endure the cold. This was needful, for the person who bought the watch at last might require a timepiece that could be trusted in all weathers and everywhere.

But some of the watches couldn't stand it; they would go too fast or too slow as the heat went up or the cold went down: they couldn't be depended on for great changes. They were marked accordingly and sent back, and the jeweller put them into cheap cases and sold them for rough-and-ready work. Other watches, however, stood the testing well; they took meekly all the changes through which they were put, and answered bravely to the regulator: these could be depended on wherever you were. These the jeweller put into rich cases—cases of gold, sometimes with costly diamonds—for they were worthy.

Every watch, you see, had a place prepared for it, just as it was prepared for the place. It wasn't by chance that one was put at last in a gold case, another in a silver one, and another in brass. Each was fitted just as it had fitted itself.

Of course there is a great difference between a watch, which can't think or help itself much, and a boy or a girl, a man or a woman, who can. Yet it is true of us, too, as it is true of the watches—the place we shall have by-and-by won't go by favouritism, and won't go by bribing, and won't go by chance, but will go exactly according to what we really are. Many a poor man will get a glorious place with the Lord, because he was a true man and faithful to his Master in everything; while many a rich man will get a very poor place, because he wasn't true and wasn't faithful. There is a place for each: every one of us must go to "his own place." What that place shall be depends on what we are now.

Mind the regulator, then, children. It is conscience —the thing that tells you when you are doing right and when you are doing wrong. Every day you will have something to try you like heat and cold. You will have temptations and vexations, and pleasures and sorrows: these are the things that test you. Keep right with conscience, then, about *everything;* never forgetting that you are being tried in Time for the place you shall have in Eternity.

XI

OUR HOME ABROAD

WALTER RIGG was an upright man, honest and true, but somewhat hard. He had his notions, and he went to church.

He was a good deal put out one day when he went there and heard a missionary speak up for Jesus and ask help for the heathen. Walter Rigg wouldn't help them—not he! They had done nothing for him, and he wasn't bound to do anything for them. Charity should begin at home. A friend at hand was better than even a brother far away. No, he felt no call to do anything for the Foreign Mission; there was enough to do at home.

That night he had a curious dream. He saw his fields withering and drying up for want of rain. He prayed, and prayed very earnestly, for rain to come; but a voice at his ear whispered to him that it was no use: the rain couldn't come, for the clouds would have to be fetched from abroad.

Then the air became so close and stifling that the blight was beginning to spring up, and he prayed for a breeze—a fresh, pure, health-giving breeze. But again the voice whispered that it couldn't come, for it would have to be fetched from abroad.

Then it became foggy and dark, and he prayed for light—sunlight, or moonlight, or starlight—anything was better than this. But he couldn't have it, the voice whispered again, for the light was so many thousand miles away.

He thought he was dying, and wondered where heaven was, and it struck him that that was far away too; and then a great fear came over him. He began to see things a little differently—to see that there was nothing that was really far away, for, one way or another, it came to be near. If there was plague or infection across the water, then as likely as not it would come here too; but if things were healthy there, there was a good chance of their being healthy here also. His foot was a good bit away from his head, but if poison got there it would soon be all over him. No, there was really no such thing as far-off or near in anything that had to do with the souls of men. The farthest away could help or hurt him, and he could help or hurt the farthest away.

He could never afterwards bear to hear anybody speak of the *Foreign* Mission and the *Home* Mission. There were not two Missions, he used to say, any more than there were two atmospheres, or two rains, or two sunshines. They were one and the same wherever they were—the Lord's one grand Mission of Mercy.

That is so—and don't you forget it!

XII

BREAKING THE SPELL

"The great trumpet shall be blown."—Isa. xxvii. 13.

Most of you have read, I dare say, the fine story of the Sleeping Beauty and the Enchanted Palace. It is long since I read it, but it is one of those stories that, once read, can never again be altogether forgotten. There was the great palace, with its far-stretching garden and its thick, shaggy woods; with its soldiers and serving-men, the little page-boys and the ladies-in-waiting. But it was all like a picture: nothing was moving; the same watchman had stood on the tower through frost and heat, as if he were a statue; the sentinel had leaned on his spear at the great gateway night and day through winter and summer, as if he had been carved out of stone; and there, in the heart of the palace, the beautiful princess and her maidens had slept and slept, while the dust of the years was falling everywhere; it was all like the grounds and the palace of a dream!

You know why: a wicked Enchanter had thrown a spell over all, and no one could lift hand or foot, or see or speak, until that spell was broken. But it could be broken if some one with faith and courage would do it. You remember how? Outside, on a tree of the enchanted wood where no fruit grew, a horn or trumpet was hung up, and beside it was a sword. Whoever would break the magic spell and awaken the sleepers, and bring all the stir and songfulness of life into that palace and these grounds again, must dare to enter the darkness of the wood, draw that sword from its scabbard, and blow a clear, loud, ringing blast on the trumpet.

And so it proved to be. A brave young knight, who had given his life for God and for all that was good, groped his way through the wood, and, in spite of all the sounds and sights that threatened him, he made his way to the tree, and drew the sword, and blew the trumpet—and then there was such a stir! The stream began to flow, the gates swung back, everybody in the palace began to move, the princess and her maidens awoke, and all the brightness and the music of life were restored.

That is a nice story, is it not? It is, and it is something more than a story; it is a parable: it only puts some big, big truths in a nice and pleasing way. For they are not palaces and gardens only that have had the spell of enchantment cast on them: whole nations have had it, and some have been under its power for hundreds and hundreds of years. They have made no progress in that time: they have had no life in them; what they were hundreds of years ago they still continued to be. The Enchanter that bound them was Superstition. But bold knights came—knights of the Cross—from the days of William Carey and John Williams, and they drew the sword, which is the Word of God, and with the breath of faith they blew the trumpet of the Gospel, and the heathen world that had long been slumbering began to awake into new life.

Oh, the great changes that have taken place within a few years, since first the knights of the Cross began to enter the darkness of heathenism! Within the memory of living men, lands that are larger than our own, and that were sunk in the deep sleep of idolatry, have cast their idols to the ground, and to-day they are as Christian as we are. Within the memory of living men, Africa was like a gloomy forest, but David Livingstone dared to enter it, and with only God's Word for a sword, but with the breath of faith with which to sound the Gospel message, he brought light and life to the Dark Continent, and now, point after point and place after place, Christian Missions are spreading all over it.

But there is one great land that has been harder to enter than most; it is a land of beauty, a land of much wisdom, too, but for longer than almost any other country it has been under the spell of superstition, so that it has made no progress; it has been as a nation asleep. It is China. Now at last, however, with the sharp sword of war and the trumpet of battle, it is being roused, and is beginning to understand that the time for sleep is over, the time for life, and all life's actions, has come. Before long that land will be thrown open from end to end for the preaching of the Gospel, as Japan was thrown open some forty years ago, and, long before your hair is grey with age, I am certain you will find that that nation, so long sunk in slumber, will be awake everywhere, and awake most of all to the power of the life that comes when Jesus is made King and Saviour.

Ah, children! that is a fine story about the Enchanted Palace and the Sleeping Princess; but it is a still finer story that is being worked out to-day in every part of the world. For the knights of the Cross are going everywhere, and everywhere the stir of a new life is going with them. When we think of what has been done in a hundred years, and then think of our steamships, and trains, and telegraphs, and printing-press, there is, I think, little need to wonder that before fifty years have fled the knowledge of Jesus the Redeemer will be brought to the whole world.

You must help; you can help. Faith first; you can pray. Pray, then, and put your heart into your prayer that Christ's kingdom may come, and that the heathen may speedily be given Him for an inheritance. Your faith, going with your prayers, will be like the very breath of life to awake the slumbering. But there is the sword, too—the Word of God; make use of that. You have your missionary-boxes—do not neglect them; they are the scabbard of the sword the missionaries have to use. Be knights of the Cross to help God's work where you are and as you are; it may be that some of you will yet yourselves go to the foreign field and be the Lord's knights there. May He grant that it shall be so! When the great victory comes—as come it must—when Christ shall be crowned King over all, look to it that this may then be your reward—that you did not hold back, but rather did what you could and as you could, to help forward the merciful work of the Lord.

XIII

CHILD-VISION

"Thou hast hid these things from the wise and prudent, and hast revealed them unto babes."—MATT. xi. 25.

THERE is such a lot of things God hides from the "wise and prudent"—from learned folk and those who think they are very clever — but which He shows to the little ones.

I don't know what a real baby sees when it is snuggled quite "comf'ably" in its cradle, but I expect it sees things a thousand times more beautiful than anything we can see. I have watched its eyes when it didn't know I was watching, and I have seen it look steadily at something in the air; then such a big, wondering look came over it, and after that there would be such a sweet, sweet smile, and then a gurgle as if the little thing were speaking a language better than my own—the language of the soul rather than that of the lips; and I have thought—What wouldn't I give to see what baby is seeing? But he is a deep little fellow; he is a foreigner, and has only come on a visit to our world, and he hasn't gone so very far into it yet but he can still see some of the glory that he came from; and he has a language of his own, different from ours, and he is not going to tell us strangers about the country of the King. He keeps that all to himself, the sly little rascal! He is a foreigner to us, but that would be nothing if he didn't treat us so provokingly as being foreigners to him, and be always bidding us to mind our own business.

Or, again, some of you little ones, have you ever looked into the fire on a quiet winter's evening? What wonderful things you have seen there! Lakes of silver and mountains of ruddy gold; armies with glittering swords, and forests thick with gloom; deep caverns where the wild beasts were crouching, and ships that sailed in the air! I have seen them all, too, so I know; and, would you believe it? I sometimes see them all yet. For I never grow old: I only kiss the years as they come, and bid them good-bye. But I keep my young eyes and my young heart still, and that is why I can talk to you.

Yes; wonderful things God reveals to the little ones, which He hides from all others. And do you know why? Just because the little ones are very simple, very trustful, and very affectionate. Yes, it all comes out of that. When we grow up we think we are bound to grow very wise and be very suspicious, and be slow to believe and quick to question, and we become very cautious, very "prudent," and we boast that we know a thing or two, and that people will have to get up very early in the morning to take us in.

What blunderers many grown-up people are, to be sure! They become proud about dust and iron, and every day they go on losing more and more of the gold and silver. Their sight grows shorter and shorter, so that they can only see the grubby things that are within arm's-length of them, and they lose sight of heaven, and the power to see one another's hearts. And they call that wisdom, or experience, or prudence! Wisdom? If that is wisdom, it has got a fool's-cap on its head! What a wise set they were in Jerusalem long ago, but they didn't know that the little Babe that was born in a manger was yet going to change all the world. And when the Apostles went about preaching the Cross, the philosophers and poets, the men who studied the stars, and the men who wrote books, all laughed at them. But who ever hears about these men now? Who even knows their names? And yet the Apostles! Why, you know them all; and, what is more, we are here to-day because their work is lasting still! But the wise and prudent saw nothing of this; they only saw the field that was being ploughed, and broken up, and sowed with seed; they didn't see the vision of the harvest that should follow. But humble folk did. God revealed to simple souls what was hidden from those who were too clever.

And that's the way He always works. It is the simple, loving, trustful heart that sees God, sees what He is doing, and sees what He is going to do. So

D

keep your hearts fresh, my bairnies, fresh and trustful and loving, all your days. Think all the good you can of other people. Try always to see the good that is in them, or the chance of the good you can do them. Keep your heart as the heart of a little child, even though you live to ninety years. It is the way to be always happy yourself; it is the way to make all others happy; and, better still, it is the way to keep the eyes of the soul clean and bright, so that they shall always be able to see what God is wanting to show.

XIV

CLEAR THE LINE!

"Seek ye first."—MATT. vi. 33.

WE are all born explorers; there is nothing we like better when we are little than to seek, and seek, and rummage about and find new places and things. Whether it is an old cupboard, or a crooked street, or a bit of a wood on the fringe of a meadow, there is a thrill of pleasure in exploring it and finding out all about it, such as we never have after discovering all that is there.

I suppose that is why every healthy boy and girl likes books of adventures and tales of travel. Oh, to have been with Columbus when first he looked on the New World! Oh, to have stood beside Magellan when his ship first glided into the silent, mighty Pacific Ocean! Oh, to be with Nansen drifting about with the icebergs on the chance of being swung round to the North Pole! But it's no use wishing; it is very nice, but it doesn't bring us any nearer. All the same we love to hear and read of the men who were the first to do things and the first to see them, and we can't help wishing for what we love; can we?

As we said, there is a bit of the explorer in us all. We like to find out, and if we are the first to find out, so much the better. And it is well that it should be so, for there isn't anything worth having but needs to be sought out, and hunted up, and asked and asked for again. That's why you are always asking "Why?" You were made to do it. You see, this is a big world, with a great many things in it, and you never saw them before or knew they were there, and so you must ask Why? Why? Why? if you are ever to find out and learn. It is a good thing, then, of itself, to have the seeking spirit.

But everything depends on how we use it, if it is to do us any good. The boy who goes seeking for blackberries, when he has been sent to seek for his little brother who has wandered away, will have a very bad quarter of an hour after he gets home. No harm, but much good, in seeking for blackberries; but much harm and no good in seeking for them when we should have been seeking for something else. And it is the same about everything; what we are doing may be right enough in itself, but it may be all wrong because we are doing it at the wrong time. There is a first and a second and a third, and very many more after these, and if we put the third second, or the second first, we have turned things the wrong way about, and are certain to suffer for it ourselves, and to make others suffer too.

What, then, is the first thing we should seek? Most people say, *Money!* Oh, to be rich! to be able to buy things, and roll about in a carriage, and live in a big house, and have tarts every day! Let me tell you a tale by a great poet.

There was a poor Roman scholar once, who was very clever and gave promise of doing much good in the world. One day he saw a strange statue with curious writing carved upon it. He could read and understand the writing, and it made him watch the shadow which the statue cast on the ground, and this led him to discover his way into a hall that was stored with riches —silver and gold and precious gems. What a quantity he gathered together! What dreams he had of the great mansion he would build and the grand things he would do! Just as he turned to go, however, he saw at his feet a wonderful green stone, and he stooped to lift it, for it was worth the price of a kingdom. But the stone was fixed to the ground, and as he struggled to loosen it he saw the figure of a knight in armour that stood near slowly lift his bow and draw the arrow on the string. The arrow struck the great jewel by which the hall was lighted, and in an instant all was dark. It was in vain the scholar groped and groped to find the door by which he had entered; he could not come by it, and so perished miserably in the dark by the side of all the treasure he had gathered together.

That is an interesting story, is it not? But what

does it mean? Just this: the riches are dear, dear, however abundant they may be, that are got at the cost of all that makes the light of life for us. They never, never should be the first.

And so there are many other things that people put first, only to find—perhaps when too late—that they should have been second, or third, or even farther down.

Jesus leaves us in no mistake. He speaks the right, clear, bold word we all need when He says, "Seek ye FIRST—!"—what? *The Kingdom of God and His righteousness.* That means—make it your *first* concern about everything to be right with God.

That fits everybody. There are some things we may never hope to be able to do: they may be too great, or too wise, or too difficult for us, or they may take too long a time, or more strength than we shall ever have. But—to be right with God!— we can all seek this, and seek successfully, too. How? By trying to live up to Jesus. He is like the top line of the copy-book, and as we imitate that, we come by-and-by to write like it. He is the Friend, and as we keep close by Him we come to speak as He speaks, and do as He does, and be as He is. What is more—He is the Helper, and when we have done wrong He can put us right. To believe in Him, to love Him and strive to be like Him—that is the first thing every one of us has to do.

I had a dream once: many have had a similar one

with the eyes open. And I saw a great many people standing before God. They were telling about all they had done. One had been a king, and had built vast palaces; another had been a soldier, and had conquered in many a battle; another had been a merchant, and had employed thousands of people; and so on. But one question was asked them: "Did you do the first thing?" One by one they hung their heads—and when I looked again they had vanished away, and there was only the sound of sobbing in the air.

Then, children, set your hearts on seeking Jesus and pleasing Him as the first thing of everything you have to do. Everything else you want and everything else you need He promises to send, and send in the right time and way, as you keep doing this. It is a promise, and Jesus never breaks His promises. Trust Him.

When the Queen has an important message to telegraph everything else has to be set aside. "Clear the line!" is the word that is then passed on, and till the royal message has been sent no other can be despatched.

That is the way this message from Jesus is sent to us. It comes saying, "Clear the line!" Everything else—books, play, work—must be second or third or fourth. "Seek ye FIRST—!" that is the command, and till we have obeyed it we have not even begun to be right with God.

So begin—now—at once. When it is a matter of life and death (as this is), of obeying God or disobeying Him, there is need that we should promptly "Clear the line!" and hearken and *do*. Seek first—seek FIRST—Jesus. "They that seek shall find."

XV

AGAINST THE STREAM

"So did *not* I, because of the fear of the Lord."—NEH. v. 15.

WOULDN'T it make a long list if we were to put down all the things we *didn't* do! What are history books made up of? Isn't it about what people *did?* These take up a good deal of space, and take some time to read, too; but if we were only told what people didn't do, the oldest man wouldn't have got through the books, though he began to read when he was a little child. No! not about even what one boy or one girl didn't do! So there is a chance for some of you, when you grow up and want to become authors and write books. Write about what people haven't done, and you will never be out of employment.

And sometimes you will have to praise them for what they haven't done, and sometimes you will have to blame them. It all depends. If they haven't done what they shouldn't have done, then that is good; but if they haven't done what they should have done, then it is bad. Everything turns on this.

Try to learn how to keep right about both these

things. How many words do you suppose there are in the big English dictionaries? Thirty-eight thousand! What a lot! To know them all would be like knowing all the leaves in a chestnut-tree in springtime. Yet, what do you think they all grow from? From two tiny little words which every baby soon learns to say—"Yes" and "No." These are the seeds; all the rest are the branches, the leaves, the flowers, and the fruits. For as soon as anybody says "Yes" or "No," then somebody else wants to know Why? or How?—and so more words have to be found to explain it all.

You must respect, then, and very much respect, these two. There is a time to say "Yes," and say it firmly, and there is a time to say "No," and say it as if you meant it. The way to know the proper time and the proper word to speak is—Remember the Lord. What would He wish? What would He do? What would He have *you* to do? Once you go by this simple rule—a rule that never fails—you will not have any difficulty in knowing the things you shouldn't do, or the things you should.

There is one time specially when you must say "No," and say it promptly, decidedly, and firmly. "*When sinners entice thee, consent thou not.*" Say "No!"—and say it in capital letters, as it were. They can't compel you; nobody can compel you to sin. All they can do is to *entice* you. You know what that means; it is coaxing, promising, tempting.

The nice bait that is put on the hook is in order to entice the fish, the crumbs that are thrown on the ground near to the trap are in order to entice the bird, and the fine promises and the glittering words sinners use are all to entice you. But the bait is useless and the crumbs can do nothing till the fish or the bird consents, and no more can other people lead you into sin till you are willing to be led. Everything depends on yourself.

There is one favourite bait you must be very watchful over. It is when they whisper to you, "What does it matter? It must be right, for everybody does it." Take care of that. If a thing is right, it is right because it is *right*, and not because a thousand people do it; and if it is wrong, it is wrong, though it were done by everybody in the world. When any one speaks to you, then, in this way, lift up your heart. Think about God—and then think about yourself. If it is wrong, *don't do it*, no matter how many may. Dare to be a Daniel: when everybody else bowed down to the image, he would not—he remembered God, and God remembered him for good. Dare to be a Joseph: when he could have sinned and got riches by it, he would not, and God made it all up to him over and over again. Dare to be like Jesus: when the tempter offered Him all the kingdoms of the world and all the glory of them if He would only fall down and worship him, Jesus would not. He dared to say No! though all the world said Yes!

Take your orders morning by morning and day by day from Jesus, and whenever you are in any doubt or difficulty, or can't quite see your way, refer the matter to the Lord, and He will give you the light you need. Be true to that light; it is sent for *you*, whatever light may be sent for others. "The fear of the Lord"—keep that uppermost in your heart, and be guided by it, and you will have the blessing of blessings—the blessing of a good conscience—as you say, "This did I," or "This did not I, because of the fear of the Lord."

XVI

IN THEIR RIGHT ORDER

"The child Samuel ministered unto the Lord before Eli."—
1 SAM. iii. 1.

THIS isn't exactly as most people would have put it. If they had seen Samuel trimming the lamps, or dusting the benches, or opening the doors, while old Eli looked on, they would have said, "The child Samuel ministered unto Eli before the Lord." They would have thought of Eli first—that Samuel was working for *him*, and attending upon *him*, while the Lord looked on. But that would have been a great, great mistake about Samuel, though it would have been true enough, unfortunately, of too many people. Samuel put the Lord first in everything, and so he did whatever he had to do as if he were doing it for God.

This is the way you must set to work, my little lads and lasses, if ever you are going to do anything right or thorough or good. One of these days, my boy, you will be leaving school, and be seeking a master. *I* wouldn't, if I were you! *I* wouldn't be like a wandering doggie asking for somebody to come and own me: not I! I would have a Master now—and such a Master as I could be always with and be always working for, and be always able to look up to and love. I would have *God* for my Master, and then, whatever I had to do, I would do it as if for Him. Isn't that better? Isn't it the right way to go to work? Ah! if we think only of an earthly master, and what will please him, we shall never do the best work. The right way is to serve the Lord before man—not serve man before the Lord.

You like stories. Here is an interesting one:—

"A new boy came into our office to-day," said a merchant to his wife at the supper-table. "He was hired by the firm at the request of the senior member, who thought the boy gave promise of good things. But I feel sure that boy will be out of the office in less than a week."

"What makes you think so?"

"Because the first thing he wanted to know was just exactly how much he was expected to do."

"Perhaps you will change your mind about him."

"Perhaps I shall," replied the merchant, "but I don't think so."

Three days later the business man said to his wife, "About that boy you remember I mentioned three or four days ago. Well, he is the best boy that ever entered the office."

"How did you find that out?"

"In the easiest way in the world. The first morning

after he began work he performed very faithfully and systematically the exact duties assigned, which he had been so careful to have explained to him. When he had finished he came to me and said, 'Mr. H., I have finished all that work. Now what can I do?' I was greatly surprised, but I gave him a little job of work and forgot all about him, until he came into my room with the question, 'What next?' That settled it for me. He was the first boy that ever entered our office who was willing and volunteered to do more than was assigned to him. I predict a successful career for that boy as a business man."

Yes, he might well do so; and why? Because that boy had evidently Samuel's spirit: he did his work as if the Lord was always looking on, even when the eye of man could not see him.

It is this way of working that helps us to do things thoroughly. You know the word "sincerity" well enough. But do you know what it really means? It means "without wax." There were dodgers in the old days as there are dodgers still, and when they had done a piece of bad work, with holes and flaws and scratches in it, they used to rub wax into the cracks and the faulty bits, and then paint them over, and so deceive their master. But could they deceive God? No; their work was a sin before Him, as all scamped work is a sin, and sooner or later their sin was sure to find them out. Be sincere, children, be sincere; let your work, whatever it is, be done as for the Lord, and you will never need putty or wax or lame excuses to conceal the faulty bits.

Think of this text whenever you are tempted to be slovenly or careless or unfaithful. It will help you to remember that all good work is sacred work. The Lord is looking on, and the Lord makes use of everything that is right and honest and good; somebody is going to be helped by it, or somebody is going to be the better for it, and so God fits it in with the things that shall last for ever and ever. If you would grow strong and true, then, and have a happy heart and do good work, keep your thoughts upon the Great Master. Whether it is learning lessons or running errands, or making or mending, let it be your rule to serve the Lord before others, not serve others before the Lord; and Samuel's portion, Samuel's power, and Samuel's greatness will be yours too, for Samuel's God will be with you.

XVII

SO TIRED!

"Jesus, being wearied with His journey, sat thus on the well."—
JOHN iv. 6.

HE was *so* tired! He had been walking on and on from the earliest morn, and seemed to be very eager about something—the disciples couldn't tell what—and the sun had risen higher and higher, and got hotter and hotter, but He still kept walking on, till now at last, when the heat was positively unbearable, He grew tired. And there was the well—Jacob's well. It was so sheltered and cool, for the trees spread their branches where the well shed its waters. So Jesus gave in at last, and sat "thus" on the well.

"Thus"! We are not told how, but there is no need. We know how tired folks rest. It is "just anyhow." A stone is very hard when you feel very strong, but when you are thoroughly worn out even a granite slab can feel as soft as hay. Jacob was very tired, you remember, and he had a stone for his pillow; but how soundly he slept! What a glorious dream he had! Ah yes, my bairnies! most things are hard or soft in this world, not because of what *they* are, but because of what *we* are. Are we tired or fresh? Are we proud or humble? Are we loving, or are we unkind? Jesus was tired—*so* tired!—and it was so restful to Him to sit on the cool grey stone!

I'm glad we are told about this. Not that I am glad Jesus was tired. Oh no! I would have spared Him if I could, and would have run His errands for Him, but yet I am glad we are told He was tired. Why? Just because there are a great many tired folk in the world, and they feel kinder to Jesus and like Him all the better for knowing exactly what it is to feel weary, weary. It so makes Him quite one of themselves!

There is a man I know something about. He printed a grand, simple book, which did people good to read. Then he printed another, called "Week-day Religion," and that, you know, is the kind of religion we need. Well, one day he got a letter from a stranger far away, saying, "Mother, sister J., and I read a chapter a day, J. usually reading aloud. It was in the spring, in house-cleaning time, and we were very weary every night. One evening J. said, 'Now for our chapter in Week-day Religion!' My feet were very tired and sore, and I said, as I threw myself on the lounge, 'I wonder what Mr. Miller knows about tired feet!' My sister replied that we should see. It was the fifth chapter—'Cure for Care' —that we were to read that evening, and perhaps you will remember that the chapter closes with the stanza in which are these lines :—

> 'And if through patient toil we reach the land
> Where *tired feet* with sandals loose may rest.'

Was not that rather a singular coincidence? I am sure that, coming as it did, it was a real word from God for me, and it brought me new strength in my weariness."

Exactly so; and that is why I like to read that Jesus was wearied. It is because it makes us know that He will understand and sympathise with us when we are wearied too.

But what happened while Jesus was resting? This: a wearied woman came to Him. She wasn't wearied exactly as He was, but she was wearied all the same—wearied of being naughty, and sinful, and bad—and wanting to find some rest for her heart, but not knowing how to get it. And here was Jesus. He could teach her how to be good and happy. Yes, but just now He was tired. Perhaps He wouldn't be troubled! Was it so? No, no. He was never so tired but He was ready to comfort and help somebody, and so He saved this woman.

That is the lesson for us. If Jesus, even when He was weary, kept on trying to do good, we must do the same. And it is the best way to get rest—by trying to put some one else at rest. Whenever you feel very weary, try to help some weaker one along, and you will yourself get fresher and stronger at every step you take. Never be weary in well-doing. That is a work that can always be carried on, for if we are tired in one way we can try another, and still be doing good. Jesus was not cross and peevish because He was tired, and neither are we except when we forget Jesus. Then keep Him in mind, and even when you feel quite worn out and weary you will still find some good to do. Happy is the boy, happy is the girl, who finds a joy in doing good to somebody else who is wearied too, though wearied, perhaps, in another way.

"Be not weary in well-doing, for in due season ye shall reap, if ye faint not."

XVIII

THE WINDING WAY

"They went up with winding stairs."—1 KINGS vi. 8.

AND you have done the same many a time, I am sure. Perhaps it was in the Round Tower at Windsor, or perhaps it was in the Monument, or to get to the dome of St Paul's. Any way, somewhere or other, some time or other, you also have gone up the "winding stairs." Then you will quite understand the feelings of the people, long, long ago, who had to go up winding stairs in the Temple before they could get to some glorious places.

They would be often very disappointed—just as you have been. You thought, didn't you? that there would only be a turn or two more in the stairway, and then you would be at the top. Was it so, however? No! Up and up, up and up, you had to go—always saying to yourself, "Another turn and I reach the last step;" but it wasn't so—there had to be another and another, and another after that, and many more again, till you began to wonder, most likely, if this was the inside of the Tower of Babel, and if you were going to touch the stars! Yes, children; that is always the way with the winding way—it is very disappointing; and that is just because it *is* a winding way, for you can only see a little bit at a time before you and above you, and sometimes you can't see even so much, for the darkness; you can only trust and feel your way, and keep going up and up, always expecting a step or two to bring you to the top, and having to expect it still.

Will you wonder if I tell you you are mounting these steps now? You are!—you are! Ask father and mother, and they will tell you the same. They have been on them—on them for a long, long time. One step was yesterday, another step is to-day, and another step is to-morrow; and so it has been with them all their lives—winding round, winding round—losing sight of yesterday as soon as it was past, never able to see to-morrow till their feet were on it, for to-morrow is always round the corner, and we have to turn to it in the dark. They will tell you, too, of a great many things they were always expecting to reach, which always seemed to be quite near, but which, somehow, have all to be mounted for yet! There was a poet once who had got an idea of these winding steps, and hadn't got the right word for them—(that has been kept for me!)—and he tried to describe it all by saying—

"Hope springs eternal in the human breast;
Man never *is*, but always *to be* blessed!"

That is just a poet's way of saying that when you are going up the winding stairs, another turn or two is always going to bring you to the end of your climbing; but it doesn't do it!

So much, I am sure, you will understand; but you will also understand that the people who went up the winding stairs of the Temple were often very tired, just as you have been. I have been so sorry sometimes for people I have seen on high, winding ways. They had no idea, when they started, that the climb would be so long or so difficult; but their hearts were not strong, and after a time they began to be faint. Then, if they stopped to rest a little they blocked the way of the sturdy ones who were coming after them, and sometimes these were very pitiless, or very selfish, or very thoughtless, and they would crush past the weak ones, or shout and say unkind things, till the poor souls have been wretched, wretched. Ah! many a time I have stood by one like that and said, "Try again! —do try—only another step or two—there!—another yet—nearly up, nearly there!—so!—keep brave—that's right!—well done!" And do you know, children, a few words of sympathy, a little help and a little cheer, have often been better than medicine or strength to help some weak-hearted one to get to the top. Mind that; and all your life be ready to give a helping hand or an encouraging word to any one who is growing weary or faint in going up the winding way. There's plenty ready to push and thrust, and have no pity;

never you be like these. It is the boy or the girl who is ready to help another up who is likest Jesus, and whom Jesus loves best.

These stairs in the Temple, however many they were, or however they went winding about, had an end at last—and then they led into such a beautiful chamber, filled with light, and so lovely to look upon that the heart was satisfied when it found rest there. How small everything in the world seemed to be as they looked down upon it from these high windows! Yes; but that wasn't the only room; another opened out from that—larger, richer, brighter, better. Ah, my bairnies! it is true—true what Jesus told us: "In our Father's house are many mansions." It may be a hard climb up the winding way, but there is a room at the top—a room for you and a room for me—which will more than reward us for all the climbing.

Then the great thing is to find the proper entrance to this winding stair, and that we are told here: "The door was in the *right* side of the house." That is very important. Do you remember what Jesus once said?—"I am the Door." There is no getting on the stairs that lead to God till we come by loving and trusting Jesus Christ. That is the *right* way; if any one comes any other way, Jesus says he is like a thief or a robber; he has taken the wrong way for the wrong purpose; he can never find welcome or blessing at the end of the winding way he has taken. So make sure about Jesus, children, at the start; it is through Him alone any of us can get on the right way, or enter the Hall of Light in peace at last. How can you do it? Why, how do you enter the doorway that leads to any winding steps? Isn't it by *faith*? You can't see all the steps that are before you; you can't see yet the beautiful rooms that are at the top, but you believe they are there, and that the steps lead to them; and so you enter the doorway in faith. Do the same with Jesus; trust Him, believe what He says, set yourself to do what He bids you; that is faith, and faith in Jesus is the way to God.

Only one other thing, children, would I like you to keep very clear in your minds. These winding stairs were a part of God's great house. That made the whole way and everything in it very sacred, did it not? Sometimes the winding way was dark, sometimes it was bright; sometimes the one who was climbing would feel strong and bold, and sometimes he would feel weak and afraid; but all the time it was the way he should go — and it was all in the Father's house. Keep that in mind, my lads and lasses, and it will help you a deal when you grow up, and have to meet with all sorts of strange things in the world. You will have joy and you will have sorrow, sad times and glad times, things you would wish for and things you wouldn't; but if you have entered by the right door, if you have put your trust in Jesus, all these things will be very good and very sacred to you, for they will all be found to help you up, higher and better, in your Father's house. Learn to look on the world and everything in it as a part of God's great house, and you will be safe there—safe, quite safe, while every day you are trying to get up higher and nearer to the room that is waiting for you—*your* place with God.

XIX

HOPING AND WAITING

"It is good that a man should both hope and quietly wait for the salvation of the Lord."—LAM. iii. 26.

HOPING and waiting—these are two of the biggest things that anybody can do, and two of the hardest to learn. But we must learn them and must do them if we would find the salvation of the Lord.

Do you know what it is to hope for a thing? It is to keep brave and expect it, even though you haven't got it yet, and there is nothing to show how you are to get it. When the farmer puts the seed in the ground in the spring-time, it is because he hopes by the end of the summer to have a great crop of wheat. But he doesn't see the wheat yet: he has not got it; he can only hope and quietly wait for it. And some days it will be very hard for him to hope. Storms will come, and floods of water will run down the furrows, and there will be fear that the seeds will be rotted away. Or snow and hailstones will fall just when the tassels are coming out, and then it will look as if there could be no harvest. The farmer is sad and troubled sometimes, but he hopes on, and at last, through all the risks and all the troubles, the autumn comes, and the harvest is gathered safe home. It is his hoping, hoping, always hoping, that keeps up his heart.

It is the same with us and everything in the world. There is a risk about it all. Yes, children, there is nothing great or grand or good in the world but you must run risks to get it. Why, what a big risk baby takes when he is good enough to come among us! He can't do anything for himself: he can't feed himself; he can't clothe himself; he can't even ask for what he wants. What a big risk he runs of being starved to death! I don't know how many diseases there are in the world, but he may catch any of them and be killed. I don't know how many sorts of accidents might occur, but any of them might happen to him. He has to risk all that. What keeps him here? What prevents him from running away back again to where he came from? It is hope: in spite of all the risks he has to run, he hopes to be able to dodge them all and get safe through.

And you? You never go through a single day without running hundreds and hundreds of risks. It is very easy for you to run out of the way of a carriage, but what if your ankle suddenly gave way? It is very pleasant to walk along the street, but what if the wind blows down a chimney-pot or slate on your head? Why, there is hardly a moment we live but we are running some risk: a sniff from a drain, a careless step, or a bit of a chill, when we are not very strong, and we are gone. What keeps us up? What helps us to live? It is hope, simple hope.

And that is how ships get over the seas and into the harbour at last. They meet with storms and calms, sunken rocks and drifting wrecks, and many other things that *might* do them harm; but they take all risk, and so they do something at last. Everything in the world is a risk, and the only thing that can keep you up is hope. So hope on, hope ever, keep a stout heart, and trust in God.

And especially about being saved. Some people are frightened to begin to go on God's way, and to say boldly that they belong to Jesus. They look along the road, and they see so many dangers, so many temptations, so many snares, that they are afraid if they begin they will never be able to end. They forget that they won't have to meet these dangers and temptations and snares all at once, but only one at a time; it is wonderful when we come to a difficulty how hope can guide us through it. So do not be afraid, children, of not getting to heaven because of anything that can happen on earth. Trust in the Lord, and hope on, hope on still. It will sometimes be hard to do it; I know things will be dark, and the road will be rough, and perhaps you yourself will be a bit weak and tired; but if your hope is in the Lord, and not in yourself, never be afraid, but go on—He will carry you through.

Hope, that is the first thing, the great thing, the heart of it all.

But *wait*—that is the next thing. "What was the hardest bit of the battle?" I asked an old soldier once who had been in a great and terrible fight. I expected him to say it was when the guns began to blaze, or when the cavalry came riding down, or when the swords were slashing wildly all around. But no! "The hardest bit of the battle," he said, "was waiting for the battle to begin." You will often find it harder to wait than to work.

The Rev. William Gray, when he was in the Alps, visited a glacier grotto that was reached by a tunnel bored through the solid ice. "As we penetrated into the chilly depths," he says, "away from the outside sunshine that flooded valley and peak, the light became dimmer and dimmer, and when we stood in the narrow chamber at the end of the passage, the darkness was as black as pitch. 'Wait,' said the guide, 'and in five minutes you shall see light clearly.' We waited, and it was just as he had told us. Yet no lamp was lit, no match was struck. What happened was this: as the eye got accustomed to its new surroundings, the atmosphere gradually brightened, the walls and the roof of the grotto glimmered into pure translucent green, and in the clear soft light that encircled us we could recognise the faces of our companions, and read the smallest type in our guide-books."

That is what waiting can do. It can open our eyes

to see things we could not see before, to see the beautiful things of God that are all around us, but which only patient, waiting eyes can see. Ah! I have known people laid aside by sickness, and known people baffled and troubled, not knowing which way to turn, everything was so dark, dark round about them; but when at last they stopped striving, and simply waited, waited on God, then the light came, and they saw God's kindness, and loved Him more and better for the quiet waiting time He pressed upon them.

So, children, though you may not know all that is in these words as father and mother know them, yet learn them, keep them in your heart, and again and again in your lifetime you will find that "it *is* good both to hope and quietly wait for the salvation of the Lord."

XX

THE MAGIC CRYSTAL

"Now we see through a glass, darkly; but then face to face."— 1 COR. xiii. 12.

WHAT a lot of things we want to know! We begin by wanting to know "how the wheels go round," and then, as we get older, we want to know how the world goes round, why it does it, and what it is all for. We want to know all about this world, and we also want to know all about the next. How are we to learn about these things? That is just what the Apostle is trying to show us.

He says we can see something about them all now, but it is darkly, as if we were looking in a kind of mirror. You children understand what he means. You read fairy tales, and poetry, and other things that are good, so you know all about Merlin and other great and wise magicians. Do you remember how they came to see things that were far away, and tell what was going to happen, and what things had been done? It was by their wonderful crystal globe.

There was the round glass ball as clear as a fountain, without a speck or a flaw, but as the magician gazed upon it it grew dim, as if the mists were going up within it; and then, as he gazed and gazed, the mists would clear away, and there, on the crystal mirror, he would see all that he wanted to know, whether it was about things far off or near, things past or things to come. 'Twas very wonderful. That crystal globe must have been long since broken or lost, for nobody has it now. It has vanished, like the magicians themselves.

But we have a mirror that is like it, though something different. It is the Bible. As we look into it reverently, lovingly, prayerfully, we see more and more, better and clearer, all we want to know about God, and ourselves; about the world, and what it is for; about life and death, and everything we need to learn. Make much of your Bible. It is the grandest possession you ever can have. Oh, the happy, happy times I have had with it in some quiet corner! What beautiful visions I have seen in it! What great things I have learnt from it! The real magician—the one who is really wise—is the boy or girl, the man or woman, who loves to look much and often into this mirror, for these come to learn there what never can be seen or learnt anywhere else—the love and the wisdom of God working through everything.

But there is another meaning this text may have. When it says we see "darkly" or dimly in this mirror, it means that it all looks like "a riddle." That is the word you find in the margin—"a riddle." And things do look like that very often. So many strange things happen we can't account for, such wonderful things are done which we can't explain, that when we look up to the stars, and then think of where we were born, and wonder where we shall die; when we see how much sorrow there is in the world, yet how much beauty and goodness too, and how things often go wrong when you meant them to go right, and how they sometimes turn out good though you never intended it, then it all looks like a riddle! Will you give it up? Some do. They grow weary, poor things, of trying to puzzle it all out. But they grow weary because they don't take the right way; that's all. How simple the most difficult riddle becomes when you have found it out! Would you like to find out this riddle?—the riddle about everything? I can tell you how. *It is by loving and trusting Jesus Christ, and trying to live like Him.* For it is said, and the word is true, "The secret of the Lord is with them that fear Him." They have the key to the riddle: everything is made simple to the one who lives loving and trusting Jesus.

Would you wish to be wise? "The fear of the Lord is the beginning of wisdom." Give Jesus your heart: learn from Him; trust Him, and He will teach you the secret of life—open up to you the good meaning of God in every dark riddle or difficulty you shall ever have to meet. So, whenever there is anything too hard for you to understand, go to Jesus, and tell Him all about it in prayer, and then, when prayer has cleansed your eyes and prepared your heart, turn to the crystal mirror of His Word: there you will get the light, the vision, the guidance you need, and so be made wise, and wiser still for His full salvation in the end, when you shall see Him, as He sees you now—" face to face."

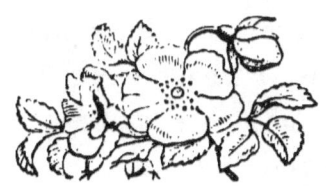

XXI

SPRING-TIME

"The flowers appear on the earth."—SONG OF SOL. ii. 12.

I CAME tramping along the quiet country lane in the sweet, sweet Easter-time, thinking many thoughts all about the busy crowded city I had left far away. I was there still. Yes; often and often when we say we shall leave all work and care behind us we are surprised to find it is not the case. Even when we are in the country our minds keep making excursions backwards and forwards to the city, without taking a railway-ticket or needing the train at all. But all at once the city was forgotten, and I was really—mind and body both together — in the country, and the country only. For there was an almond-tree before me with all its blossoms out, and it stood against a ploughed field where everything was bleak and bare, as much as to say, "The Spring has come! oh yes, the Spring has come! My banners are out, and these brown fields will soon be green, and the gardens will soon be gay! The Spring has come!"

So I watched for the Spring as I tramped along.

The road was thick with dust—grey dust—for it was a chalky land, and the east wind was blowing, keen but kind, while the sun was scattering the warm gold everywhere. I looked on the hedges, and saw the Spring had been there before me, for tiny green buds were dotted all over them, but the Spring had left no footprints in the dust. I looked through the railings of a great wide garden, and there were the crocuses, like little shootlets of flame; and snowdrops, like winter's leavings; and primroses—oh! the primroses!—and daffodils!—and the red currant was taking its tint, and the willow in the corner was putting out its fuzzy burrs—so I knew the Spring had come there.

As I went on the dusty road again I looked into the hedge-banks on the sunny side, and there they were—my sweet little pets come back again—the celandine, the wild hyacinth, shepherd's purse, the speedwell, and oh, so many more!—and I knew the Spring must have strolled along this road before me. There was no fence round the little patch in front of the poor widow's cottage, and there was an ugly little shrub, squinting every way, as if it were always afraid of being pulled up and thrown away, yet the green buds were starting all over it; and on the window-sill there was an old cracked pot with a cowslip coming up—the one that had been planted by the poor lame boy who had lived with the old woman for a week last summer. The Spring had kissed it too and made it beautiful as she passed!

I strolled along very slowly after that, for I had now a great many thoughts to carry with me. The Spring was everywhere, and everywhere it was like God Himself. Wherever it came it brought life and beauty. It made no difference: it made the rich man's garden beautiful, but it left a blessing also on the poor widow's bit of ground; it made the sap rush strong and glad in the great tall trees, but it also touched with a kindly touch the root that the little lame child had planted. It made no difference: wherever there was that which wanted it, there it came, and came with a blessing.

That is just the way with Jesus Christ. He makes no difference between high and low, or rich and poor, or young and old—everybody is dear to Him alike; and wherever there is any one who wants Him, there He comes, and then the spring-time of that soul has begun. You can always tell where He has been, just as you can tell when the Spring has come. The signs are the same. First there is *life*—new life—a life that grows upward and seeks for the light. Where the heart was cold before it now becomes loving and warm; and the prayer goes up from it now as fragrance goes from a flower. Wherever Christ comes the soul begins to live in the love of God.

After that, of course, there comes *beauty*, which is the blossom of the praying soul. It is a beauty like Christ's own—the beauty of pure thoughts and loving deeds; the beauty of patience, and of truthfulness, and of charity; the beauty of the Lord Himself, who has loved it into life. And then, of course, by-and-by, there comes the *fruit*. The leaves are beautiful, the flowers are beautiful; but they are all meant to get things ready for fruit in the autumn. The fruit is everything, and that is how it must be with us all at the last.

Children dear, this is the Spring-time with you. You are young, you are little; but in every one of you there is a heart Jesus loves and wants to be loved by again. Whose shall it be?—His or yours? Will you keep it for yourself, or will you say, "Dear Lord, take it and keep it for Thyself"? Say that and mean it, and the Lord will put His blessing on it—the blessing of life; and when the spring has passed, and the summer has gone, and the autumn has come, all the fruit shall be gathered for eternity, and it shall be all yours—all yours—just because it is all Christ's too.

The Lord is near you now; may He hear every heart wish for His blessing!

XXII

SOWING AND REAPING

"A sower went forth to sow."—MATT. xiii. 3.

JUST so: and it might have been you or me! For everybody is sowing seeds of one sort or another, even when he doesn't know it. How are the tiniest islands on the loneliest seas covered with grass and trees and graceful ferns and creeping plants? Because the bees and the birds have carried seeds with them when they didn't know it. And whether we mean it or not, we are always planting something, and that something grows. If we have planted what is bad, bad will come of it; if we have planted what is good, good will come of it. The good or the bad things which we speak and do are the seeds we are sowing,—and they grow!—they grow!

The first thing, then, we must look to is—to choose good seed. We can have it: it is all stored up for us in God's Book—for every good word it gives us, every kind thought it puts into our heart, everything it says which can cheer and help us and cheer and help others, all that is good seed which God gives. Then we must sow it, and must try to sow nothing *but* it.

Let me tell you something which perhaps you don't know. *The best time for sowing is when the mist is on the ground.* The wisest sowers will tell you this. They don't see where the seed is falling, but they scatter it about; they know that the mist which hides from them where the seed has fallen is yet a very kindly, motherly mist, which will kiss the seed with moist and loving lips, and kiss it into life. And so they sow—*in faith.*

You must learn to do the same. Be kind wherever and whenever you get the chance, not only to the people you know and meet with at home or school, but also to strangers and the poor folk you must meet everywhere. Sow your seed in the mist: "scatter seeds of kindness" even when you can't see where they are going: sow in faith, just for Jesus' sake, and one day, when the mists have all vanished, and the sun is bright, and the Beautiful Day of God has come, angel upon angel will pass you by with a golden sickle in his hand and a goodly sheaf pressed to his bosom, and with a smile he will whisper as he goes up to God: "This is yours, all yours, and yours for ever, for it was your hand that sowed the good seed."

What a reward for faith! What a wonder! What a blessing! Then "scatter seeds of kindness": do it in faith: do it for Jesus' sake. When the harvest comes your heart will be rich—rich beyond anything you can dream of now.

XXIII

YOU AND I AND EVERYBODY

"A wise man's heart is at his right hand: but a fool's heart at his left."—ECCLES. x. 2.

YES, I know what you want to do! You want to slip your hand about to find where *your* heart is! And the old folks want to do it too, only they are a little afraid of what they might discover. It is perfectly astonishing, when you come to think of it, how few people know where their heart really is. Most business men, when they mean to lay their hand on their heart, put it on their pocket-book, and, strange to say, they generally carry that on the left side! That's somewhat odd, is it not? considering what this text says. And there are some ladies who never speak about their heart without smoothing their dress, or stroking their gloves, or touching up their hair— as if they weren't quite sure where their heart was. And perhaps they are not, for a lady's heart is very peculiar; it even gets lost sometimes—and so the text doesn't venture to say anything at all about it. It speaks only about the heart of a wise *man* and the heart of a foolish one.

Where are these placed? There it is, as plain as print: "A wise man's heart is at his right hand: but a fool's heart at his left." Now try where yours is. I know where mine is, and it makes me blush a bit to acknowledge it, but I really can't help it. My heart is on the left side! Where is yours? On the left side too? And yours? and yours? and yours? What? not one of us got his heart on the right side, where a wise man's heart must be! That *does* take the conceit out of us, does it not? Not one wise person among us! It *is* rather a take-down.

But did you ever meet anybody yet who had his heart on the right side? *I* never did, and I don't think you ever did either. Everybody has his heart on the left—there or thereabouts. When you meet with the one who has his heart on the right side, you may consider yourself fortunate, for then, but not till then, will you have met with a person who is perfectly wise.

That is just what the text wants to teach us, and teach us in a quiet, kindly way, with a little twinkle in the eye, as it were, while it is speaking. It wants us to understand that there is nobody perfectly wise; there is a good deal of foolishness in everybody.

Some people know this, and some people don't— and these are the most foolish of all. That is the kind of person the next verse speaks about. Hear what it says:—"Yea, also, when he that is a fool walketh by the way, his wisdom faileth him, and he saith to every one that he is a fool." We have sometimes seen people like that; people that hold their heads very high, and who think a great deal of themselves, and who look down on everybody else as being very foolish—very foolish indeed—while all the time the fool's-cap is on their own head, and everybody sees it but themselves.

Then, children, this is what we must learn :—

(1.) That there is nobody perfectly wise. You are not, I am not, the oldest isn't, and even the youngest has something yet to learn. Get that lesson well off, then you will be ready for the next.

(2.) To be very strict about yourself, and very charitable about other people. It is very amusing to hear the pot call the kettle black, but it is very sad to see one foolish person despising another. The boy in the top form may know a good deal more than the boy in the lower one, but he has yet a lot to learn before he can come up to the master. Conceit always proves ignorance, for it shows you are measuring yourself by somebody who hasn't had a chance to know better, rather than by somebody who has learnt a great deal more than you have. So be charitable and make allowances for people, for every day, though you may not know it, somebody has to make allowances for you. Don't waste your time in trying to find the perfectly wise man or boy. You won't find him; no, not even when you look in the mirror!

(3.) Then, be humble. Though there is a good deal

of foolishness in every one, never forget that there is a good bit of wisdom too. I never met a person yet who couldn't teach me something I never knew before and that was well worth the learning. Try to find that out; if it is only a little gem in a bushel of dust, you will be richer and better for searching it out. Be ready to learn from everybody, by never forgetting that your own heart also is on the left side.

(4.) And the best way to carry this humble, kind, and charitable heart, so as really to grow wiser and wiser every day, is by always looking up and keeping mind of Jesus. He alone is the all-wise One, and yet how He puts up with us and our foolishness day after day! Ah! when we think of Him we have all to hang our heads very low. Then think of Him, and think much of Him, for the humble head makes the wise heart at last, for it makes us loving, and pitiful, and helpful to everybody. Whenever you are tempted, then, to think proud, conceited, or hard and uncharitable thoughts about anybody, just find out where your own heart is, and it may help to make you kinder and better—and more like Jesus.

XXIV

GIVING AND GETTING

"All things come of Thee, and of Thine own have we given Thee."
—1 CHRON. xxix. 14.

Down at the foot of the great hills there was a little hollow in a valley; no grass grew there, for the clay was hard, and the ground was very dry. But there came a cloud, and it hung over the hollow, and dropped down its rain upon it, and filled it. And the hollow was so pleased, so glad, and so thankful, because now it was no longer empty. And the sun came forth and asked for a drink, and the little pool gave it gladly, though it had now less water than it had before. But the clouds came over it again and filled it—fuller than ever—and the sun returned and asked for a drink, and the pool gave it gladly and brightly again—glad that it had something to give to the sun.

And so it went on, day after day, month after month, and the clouds filled the pool, and the pool gave from its fulness to the sun, till the pool became larger and larger, and became a great lake. Then it grew proud and haughty because it had now become great, and one day, when the sun asked again for a drink, the lake said, "No, I cannot afford it. I want to keep all that I have to myself till I become like the sea." And the sun turned away its beams, and there was no longer any sparkle or brightness on the water; and the clouds hovered above it, but drifted away, and dropped no more rain; and the lake grew stagnant and foul, and the beautiful things that had been living in it died away one by one; and the lake that had been so bright and happy was wretched and miserable. It called to the brooks, but they said they could not help it—they could only give what the clouds gave to them. Then it called to the clouds, but they said they could do nothing for it—they could only give what the sun gave to them, and could only give it where the sun commanded them.

Then the poor stagnant little lake found out that all that it had it had got through the kindness of the sun that made the clouds. Oh, how sorry, sorry—how ashamed was the lake then at what it had done in refusing to give a drink to the sun that had given it all that it had!

That is the story, children; I leave you to find out the meaning yourselves; only saying this: All things come from God, and what we give to Him we can give only because He has first given it to us, and all that we keep back from Him when He asks us to give always works harm, and evil, and loss for us in the end. It is as we give to God we get from God; as we honour Him He honours us.

XXV

LAMP AND OIL

"They that were foolish took their lamps, and took no oil with them: but the wise took oil in their vessels with their lamps."—MATT. XXV. 3, 4.

WHICH is worst—a lamp without oil, or oil without a lamp? It is not easy to say off-hand. The lamp may be very beautiful, very costly, very fine, but if there is no oil in it there can be no light, and that is the point. On the other hand, the oil may be the very best, the very purest, and the very clearest, but if you have nothing to keep it in and draw it properly to the wick, you can't have a steady light to help you along the road. Of course, you could set fire to the oil itself and have a big flare-up, but that wouldn't do for any one who wants to pick his way along a dark road, or guide others, or take part in a happy procession.

Both are bad—the lamp without the oil, and the oil without the lamp. There is a question tiny little children are often asked, because grown-up folks think it will puzzle them. "Which do you like best, father or mother?" And you know how cleverly the little mites wriggle out of the difficulty: they look from the one to the other and the other to the one, and then say, "I loves *bos* best!" And that is quite right, and it is what we must do with the lamp and the oil, the oil and the lamp—we must love both best. They are useless when they go apart, but they are beautiful when they go together. We are commanded by Jesus to let our light shine, and we can never do that properly in the world unless we have a good lamp, and good oil in it too.

The lamp is the *form* and the oil is the *life:* the lamp is the *body*, the oil is the *soul:* the lamp is what we are *like*, the oil is what we *are*—but I am afraid this is very learned: I must make my meaning simpler.

When I was at college we had a very beautiful man among us. (It is so odd, is it not? to speak about a "beautiful" man. It is all right to say that a lady is beautiful, or a flower, or a bird: but a *man!*—a "beautiful man!"—why, it is like making fun of him. A man should be strong, or handsome, or wise, or brave; but *beautiful!*—pah!—let us leave that to the girls!) But this was a beautiful man—very. On great days, when the public were invited, we always made him sit in front for a specimen, as it were, of what we were all like! He called himself a student, but he never studied: he was at college to learn wisdom, but he never grew wise. He made fun for us all when he didn't intend to, for the more he tried to show his learning, the more his ignorance would come out. We called him The Lamp, he was such a fine vessel; but there was no oil in it: he didn't shine then, and has never shone since. He was a real fine fellow otherwise, only he wasn't a student while he seemed to be one—and when you seem to be one thing while you really are another, you are only a lamp without oil.

But there was another student we had, as plain as plain could be, with a bit of a crook in his body besides, and he *was* a student. He had more learning in his little finger than most of us had altogether. He was very warm-hearted and impulsive, very brave, and thoroughly honest and sincere, but very dirty, very slatternly, and very often very, very rude. He never cared what he said or what he did; he meant well, and his heart was good, but he had a great contempt for appearances. Of course he was always getting into trouble for doing right things in a wrong way. He died, poor fellow, and we nursed him tenderly to the last, taking our turns to sit up with him night and day; for we all loved the warm-hearted fellow-comrade, though we were always afraid of what he would do next. He was the oil without the lamp, and soon burnt himself out, without doing half the good he wished to do and might have done, if he had only considered the value of the lamp—the form and appearance of things.

As you grow up you will meet many people like these. Do you not meet them now? Isn't there a boy you know who is very proper, very good-mannered, very correct, but very selfish and greedy and unkind?

He is a lamp without oil. And do you not know the boy who is very ill-mannered, very boorish and clownish and rude, but very warm-hearted and obliging and loving in his own way? He is the oil without the lamp. A real gentleman is lamp and oil together—good manners and a good heart both.

There are other ways besides in which we require the lamp as well as the oil. There is *reverence*, for example. I knew a little boy who reasoned this way about his prayers:—"I don't need to kneel down; I can pray just as well standing." And so he said his prayers anyhow while getting ready for bed. After a while he said, "I can pray just as well after I am in bed as before"—and he did. But for how long? Not very long: he soon got into the habit of going to sleep without prayer at all, or any thought of Jesus. He became, in fact, prayerless. The oil did not burn very long after the lamp was thrown away. Keep up the forms of reverence, children: they help you more than you can guess. It is all very well to have the soul of religion, but a soul must have a body, or be a mere ghost, just as the oil must have a lamp, or be a mere flash; and the better the oil is, the better the lamp should be; and the more we love God, the more we should show it by our reverence in everything that has to do with Him. Never speak lightly of things sacred; never deal lightly by them. Never be late for church if you can help it; reverence will always wait there for the Lord, rather than keep the

Lord waiting there for it. Do not be, however, like the foolish virgins, who had plenty of reverence but no love for the Lord; who had beautiful lamps but no oil in them. Be like the wise virgins, who had both reverence and love; who brought their lamps, but brought oil with them too. Only these went in with the Lord to the banquet. Do not be left out. Let your light shine, then, and shine brightly, by having faith, but works too; by having love, but reverence with it also — by having oil and lamp both.

XXVI

A QUESTION OF TASTE

"Is there any taste in the white of an egg?"—JOB vi. 6.

NONE whatever! There is *no* taste in the white of an egg. That is—if it is "sound." If it is a bit "high," however, there *is* a taste in it—and a nasty taste, too! We won't speak of that; 'tisn't pleasant. Eggs of that sort are not for eating; they are only good for contested elections, though I don't hold by them, even then!

Speaking of good, sound, healthy eggs, however, you have all noticed that there is no taste in the "white." There is in the yellow "yolk"—but we are not speaking of it. I don't suppose there is one of you but has made the remark at the breakfast-table that there was no taste in the "white," and I have no doubt that you thought it was a very original observation. Yet here is a man who had said the same thing more than three thousand years ago! That is discouraging; it always is discouraging to find your original remarks are only echoes of what somebody else has said long before. Not to be able to say even a thing like this without finding that it had been said before the Pyramids were built—this is enough to take the very heart out of genius. The only way I can think of for escaping these humblings is by never pretending to be original at all. But as it isn't given to everybody to be as wise as this, we must just put the best face on things we can.

Any way, it is quite true that there is no taste in the white of an egg. If it were a mere matter of "taste," I would have nothing more to say about it, for everybody has his own taste like his own nose, different from everybody else's. You like one thing, I like another, and the boy round the corner likes something neither of us can bear. When it is only a question of taste in that fashion, there is no use arguing; everybody has his own.

But everybody is agreed about this. That's something. Now, what is the white of an egg? It is the chick's rations! Yes. It is something within the "yolk" which makes the chick, and as soon as he gets a beak he begins, naturally, to feel peckish a bit, and so he makes for the "white." By the time he has eaten that up he has grown so big and so important that he disdains the world within the shell in which he was reared, and steps out into this larger world, and gets introduced to relations he hadn't had the pleasure of meeting before. Then he forgets all about the "white,"—yet if it hadn't been for the white he would have died of starvation in the shell, as completely as ever an Arctic traveller died among the icebergs through want of food. It is too bad of him to forget; but it is the way of chickens.

The thing for us to notice is, that though the "white" has no taste it has very great strength. It is food for the chick, and it is food for you and me. Everything that is needed to make bone and blood and feathers—or hair—is in the white of an egg. Yet it is tasteless! Then that shows, does it not? that there are things in the world that are very good for us even though they may not be as pleasant as sugar or as quick to be noticed as some of the medicines the doctor gives us! They are tasteless, but they are strengthening—that's the point—the first point at least.

The next point is this—the only way to find out how good these tasteless things are is by *taking* them. I have often seen the white of an egg exhibited in the chemistry class of a morning, and a great many wonderful things were done to show what it was made of, and how it was hardened, or softened, by this thing and that; but if any poor student had come there without his breakfast, he might have been made wiser, but he wouldn't have been made any stronger, by all he learnt. There is only one way of getting the strength that is in the white—and that is, by eating it.

As I said, then, there are a great many things like it in this respect; they are tasteless, but good. There is *Duty*, for example. Not much taste about *it!*

There is a fine smack about *pleasure;* merely to look on it is enough to make the mouth water; but *duty!*—ah! there isn't much spice about it. To have to do the same thing over and over again just because it has to be done, and not because we like to do it, is very tasteless work. But what strong men and women it makes! There is nobody strong who shirks his duty, and there is nobody weak who has got into the habit of doing it. The best soldiers, the best sailors, the best men and women everywhere, are those who have learnt to do their duty for duty's sake, and not because there is anything sweet about it to tempt them on. Strengthen yourselves here, my bairnies. Whatever you ought to do, *do* it—just because you ought, and though it is as tasteless at first as the white of an egg, it will make you at last stronger than Samson.

Another very tasteless thing is—singing sweet songs to a saddened heart. Let me explain. Sometimes people become very sad; some one they have dearly loved has died, or they have been greatly disappointed, or some one has done them a wrong, and their hearts are heavy. They care nothing then for the sweetest songs. Everything they delighted in before becomes to them then as tasteless as the white of an egg. All the same they are the better for the songs and better for the sympathy. They don't feel it at the time, but yet it puts new strength into them; just as with the white of an egg. Speak kindly to the sorrowing, speak hopefully to the sad; though they don't seem to listen or care for what you say, yet they are all the better for it, and will be better for it still. Even sympathy and kindness can be tasteless at times; but they are always strengthening.

And there is *worship*. What a pity that should ever be tasteless! But sometimes it is. Sometimes a person finds no pleasure in going to God's House, hearing His Word, or singing His praises. Sometimes he has no pleasure even in praying! Think of that! How you would wonder at yourself if your heart didn't dance and your eyes didn't brighten when you met somebody you really loved! You would say, would you not? that there was something wrong with yourself then. You would, and you would be quite correct; and it is just the same with us all when we cease to find any pleasure in meeting with Jesus in worship or praise or prayer. The fault is in ourselves; we have lost our taste. People do so sometimes. When they are sick or ill or out of sorts there are many things they don't care for, of which they were very fond when they were in health. And the doctor tests them by it. He asks them from time to time, "Can you take this yet?" or, "Do you like that?" and so he knows whether they are getting better or getting worse. We can tell about our own hearts, our own spirits, in the same way. If we have no pleasure in meeting with Jesus, in praising Him or praying to Him, it is a sure sign there is something wrong with us. There is sin somewhere, and it is making the soul sick and weak. There is no hope for us then unless that sin is put away. Till that is done we shall blame the worship, blame the praise, blame everything and everybody but ourselves; just as the sick man does when he has lost his taste. Yet the fault is in ourselves all the time!

Then, children, when you don't like to go to church, don't like to praise Jesus, don't like to pray to Him, just give a look into your own heart and you will find something wicked there. Put that away; ask Jesus to pardon it, and the things that seemed so tasteless before will be found to be very pleasant, and, what is more, they will be found to be very strengthening, like the white of an egg. Water is tasteless when you are not thirsty, and bread has no flavour when you are not hungry, but how sweet water is when your tongue is parched! and how toothsome bread is when you are ready to perish! There is no spice like hunger and thirst. When you come to Jesus bring the hunger and thirst with you, and I promise — nay, Jesus promises, you shall be abundantly satisfied.

XXVII

A NARROW ESCAPE

"Be ye thankful."—COL. iii. 15.

HE was a nice lad, going home for the holidays after having been away for a year at his first situation; and the old gentleman who sat opposite him in the carriage was a kindly, friendly sort of a man; so the two soon got into conversation and talked about many things. George was in a very impatient mood; the train was steaming along at a fine rate and doing its very best, but it was going too slow for George; he wanted to fly and be home. So he grumbled—grumbled at every stoppage, and whenever the train had to go slow because the signals were against it, George used up almost every growling word in the dictionary. The old gentleman with the kindly, gentle face listened to his grumbles with a twinkle in his eye or a good-humoured smile on his lips; he had been young himself once, and had been from home, and knew what it was to want to be quickly back, but in his young days they had to travel by stage-coach, and that was a good deal slower than a goods-train now.

At length, however, they came to a junction, where

they had to change. George fretted about this a good deal, for they had seven minutes to wait before the train that would take him home came up; but no sooner had the old gentleman stepped on the platform than he said, very simply, but very thoughtfully, "Thank God!" George thought it a strange thing to say, and to say so prayerfully, too, but he made no remark about it, and by-and-by the two started off again in the same carriage; they were both bound for the same place. Before they had run many miles, however, they heard their engine whistle sharply, "Down brakes! down brakes!" and as they looked out of the window they saw the reason. Something had gone wrong with a switch, and their train had been shunted on the wrong line, while there—ahead of them on the straight cutting—they could see another train rushing straight for them. Jerk, jerk, jerk went their train, and grind, grind, grind went the wheels beneath them. It was a terrible moment, and George's face was very white. Within a few yards of one another, however, both trains stopped; then the one that had got on the wrong line backed out, and the other went slowly and cautiously past.

"Thank God!" said George very earnestly, for he was a good lad; "that *was* a narrow escape!"

"It was," said the old man quietly; "and I am glad to hear you thank God."

"Weren't *you* frightened?" George asked, wondering at his quietness.

"Well, yes, I was," said the old man, "frightened a good deal, and I thank the Lord heartily along with you that He has saved us from harm. But don't you think," he added, "that you ought to have thanked Him, too, when you got safely to the last junction where we changed? Ah, my lad, my lad," he said gently, "don't be like the most of people, who thank God only when they have escaped from some danger they have seen. It is better, it is manlier, it is worthier to thank Him when He hasn't so much as let us see the dangers from which He has been keeping us. There isn't a moment that He isn't protecting us; if He were to lift His shield from round us for an instant, we would be cut down by sickness, or hurt by accident, or killed outright. Now, which is best—to thank Him for keeping us from even seeing danger, or to thank Him only in the rare times when He gives us a glimpse of what might have happened but for His care?"

"You are right, sir," said George; "it is best to be always thankful." And George learned a lesson that day he never forgot.

Will you learn it too? Learn to thank God prayerfully for what hasn't happened, as well as for what has? Do so, and you will never be without a song and a sunbeam, for these always are given to the thankful spirit.

XXVIII

ROOM AND POWER TO LET

"I am not ashamed of the gospel of Christ: for it is the power of God unto salvation, to every one that believeth."—Rom. i. 16.

No, you need never be ashamed of the gospel, children; nobody needs ever be ashamed of glad tidings—and that is what the gospel is and what it means—glad tidings about salvation.

We can't save ourselves: let us be perfectly clear about that. I once went down the deepest mine in England to preach the gospel to the pitmen. It was such a queer thing to be away down there in the heart of the earth, with a block of coal for a pulpit, and half-naked men all about me, and guttering candles and miners' lamps twinkling in the darkness. When we got on the cage again to come to the top, a friend took hold of my arm as if *he* would lift me up; but we never moved—we got no higher: he had no power to lift me; I had no power to lift him. We had both to wait till the signal was given, and the great engine overhead, which we could not see, put out its power and drew us up. That is a mistake people are always making: they think they can save themselves or save one another. They can't. You might as well try to lift yourself by grasping your own shoulders as try to save yourself by anything that you can do. Only the power of God can save us.

One of the greatest preachers this country ever had was Whitfield—a man who brought many, many to God, that they might be saved. He had a brother, however, whose heart was very heavy and whose life was very sad, because he feared he was lost. Lady Huntingdon spoke to him one day about how ready God was to pardon and save the greatest sinner. "Ah, yes," he said; "but there is no mercy for me. I am lost, entirely lost!" "I am glad of it," said Lady Huntingdon; "very glad indeed to hear it." The man was astonished. "What!" he asked, "are you glad to hear that I am lost?" "Yes, indeed I am," she said, "for it is written that Jesus Christ came into the world to save the lost." How that word went home to the heart of the man! He had never seen it that way before. "I thank God for that word," he said, "and now I trust my soul into His hands." A few months afterwards, feeling unwell, he went out into the open air, where he fell in a faint, and was carried back to the house, and soon died. Yes, but he was saved: saved because, as one who was lost, he had trusted himself altogether to Jesus Christ, who came into the world to seek and to save the lost.

This is where we must begin if ever we would be saved: we must let Jesus save us: we cannot save ourselves. Only the power of God can do it, and that power comes through Jesus Christ.

There is a curious notice that is sometimes seen stuck up on great buildings in Yorkshire and other places in the North. It is this—"ROOM AND POWER TO LET; *Apply within.*" These are the two things everybody wants—room and power. One of these days, when you leave school, you will be wanting room—some opening, some situation, in which to find your work. That is why the emigrant goes abroad, leaving his native land and all his friends—he wants to find room, more room in which to till the soil and sow his seeds and raise his crops than he can find at home. When we are little we all dwell snugly enough under the one roof, but when we grow up the place becomes too small for us all, and so, as the little birds have to be pecked out of the nest, by-and-by we have all to be pushed out into the world to find room for ourselves. The first thing we have all to find, if ever we would do any work in the world, is—*room*. And the next is *power*. Everybody wants that. Kings go to battle for it; men and women scramble over one another for it: if they can only get into power there are people who are willing to part with everything that is good, and beautiful, and lovely, and true. Some want it very sadly. The sick child lying so weak and helpless wishes for power to get up, and mother wishes she had power to give him. The man who has gone all wrong wishes he had power to get right again, but though he tries and tries, his heart is like to break at times when he finds there is such a difference between wishing and having. We all wish we had power—power to do this or power to do that—but sometimes the more we wish for it, the more we are made to feel that we haven't got it. And yet there is room and power to let! I think we had better apply "within," to find out what this means. Once we have got inside it all becomes simple enough. There are a number of rooms where every man may bring his own machine, his turning-lathe, or his loom, or whatever it is, and fit it up; then all he has to do is to join his machine by the leather band with a great revolving shaft which passes through all the rooms, and he has got the power he needs. There are many rooms and many different kinds of work going on in them all, but they are all driven by the same engine—the engine that turns the great shaft. Though nobody sees that engine, everybody believes in it, trusts to it, and knows how strong it is—by what it can do.

It is the same with us, children, and the power we need for salvation. That power must come from God. But it is there, it is free, it is offered to us—and that is what makes up the gospel of Jesus Christ. Yes, and the glad news is all about Jesus coming to be a Saviour. The angels preached it first. "Behold," said one of them, "I bring you good tidings of great joy, which shall be to all people. For unto you is born this day in the city of David a Saviour, which is Christ the Lord."

Glad tidings—and a Saviour—that *is* the gospel. And another angel said, "Thou shalt call His name Jesus; for He shall save His people from their sins." *He* shall do it! What we could not do ourselves Jesus came to do for us. Ah, children! be clear about this—there is only one way to be saved, and that is through the power of God; and Jesus Christ has that power. His is the kingdom, and His the power, and His is the glory.

Then the first thing we need to do is to join our hearts to the heart of Jesus. It doesn't matter how beautiful the machine may be that is fitted up in one of those rooms we spoke of, it can't go, it can't work, till the gearing-band is on it that brings it under the power of the great, strong engine. And it doesn't matter how clever we are, how wise, how well educated or kind we may be, if we don't bring our hearts under the power of God we cannot be safe.

The gearing-band that joins our hearts to Christ is *faith*. The gospel of a Saviour is the "power of God unto salvation to every one that *believeth*."

There is such a difference between knowing and believing. A man may know all about the driving engine and all about his own machine, but till he joins the two together there is no power. And you may know all about Jesus, all about the Bible, and all about the way of being saved; but if you don't trust Jesus, believe on Him, so as to live by Him, He can't help you; *can't*. You know something of how great the Lord's power was when He was on earth; He could heal the sick, give sight to the blind, make the deaf hear and the dumb to speak, and could even bring the dead back into life again. Yes; but there was a time when He could do nothing: "He could do no mighty work." And why? "Because of their unbelief." It doesn't matter how strong the engine is, if you don't connect it with your machine it can't help you. Did you ever find this text in the Bible, "Know about the Lord Jesus Christ, and thou shalt be saved"? You never did. Or this one, "Hear about the Lord Jesus Christ, and thou shalt be saved"? You never did. This is what you find, "*Believe* on the Lord Jesus Christ, and thou shalt be saved."

Would you wish to be saved? Then believe in Jesus—trust Him, just trust Him. That is a very simple thing to do, is it not? It is; and it is a very simple thing to slip on the gearing-band of the machine, but how great is the power that comes by doing it! And the power of God is greater still. How quietly it comes, and yet how wonderfully it works! A little while ago and the earth was cold and black, and the trees were bare, and the seeds were dead in the ground; but God put out His power, and how changed everything has become! The trees have budded, the seeds have been made alive, the flowers are blooming, and the beautiful life of the spring-time is all about us.

Yet it was all done so quietly—without noise or any startling suddenness. And that is how His power for salvation works in our hearts when we set our trust on Jesus Christ. A spirit of power passes upon us, better, stronger, grander than our own. It is the power of God, and what we could not do with our own power we can do with God's. Try it—try it just as the disciples did at the first. When Jesus was going away from them—going up into heaven—they were very sad. They wanted to be saved, and to be saved for something—saved to live right and true and beautiful lives, for the love of God and for love of man—but they were afraid they would not be able to if Jesus went away. But He told them not to fear; He was going away to receive all power, and He would send power to them; and they believed Him. They could not tell how it was to be done, but they believed Him; and they just waited and prayed, and prayed and waited, and one day the power of God came upon them, and after that, oh! the great and good things they did, which they could not have done of themselves. It was the Lord Himself working through them—just as it is the power of the great engine that works through the machine that is joined to it. And you will find it the same as you take the same way of joining your heart to the heart of Jesus Christ. Wait and pray, pray and wait, and pray again. He has given a promise, and for Him to give a promise is for Him to keep it; and the promise is this—to give the Holy Spirit to every one

that asks it. Ask Him—ask Him with your heart—
and the power you need, the power of God unto
salvation, will pass upon you, and you shall be saved.
Oh, what a grand thing that is!—to be able to walk
through the world and face its dangers, and meet its
temptations and all its ups and downs, and yet know
that you are saved—that the power of Christ is on you,
—that you belong to Him, and He will never, never let
you be lost. This is to live the true life, for it is the
life that shall live for ever and ever.

Sometimes you will find it hard to be good and hard
to do good. You may have the will and may have the
wish, but somehow you will feel you haven't the power.
It is the same sometimes with some of those machines
we have been speaking about. They are joined by a
leather band with the great, strong, whirling shaft above,
but yet they are moving very slowly, and often stop
and are not doing much work. And why? Because
they have let the band that joins them to the shaft
become slack. What they are needing is more power,
and they cannot receive that until the band is made
firmer and tighter; and that is what we need to do
when we find it hard to be good, and hard to do good.
We need to tighten the band that joins us to Jesus.
We need more faith. On one occasion Jesus was
telling His disciples how to be loving—very loving.
If anybody had vexed or wronged them and was
afterwards sorry for it, they were to forgive him, and
forgive him again and again, and yet again. And they

found that a very hard thing to do. But Jesus said they were to do it, and that was enough for them; so all they wanted now was to find out *how*. And what do you think they asked for? More love? No, but more *faith*. "Lord," they said, "increase our faith." They believed in Jesus; they knew that He had power enough to help them to do whatever He commanded them; so all they asked for was, to make the band tighter—to increase their faith—that through more faith they might receive more power. That is the way for you and me and everybody. What we cannot do Jesus can, if only we will trust Him more and make the band of faith a little firmer, so as to draw more power from Him.

Then look well to the gearing-band. Be often in prayer—often: morning and night upon your knees, and during the day a little thought, a little word, send up to Jesus. And listen for Him. He speaks through the Bible, telling us what He wants us to do—what He has saved us for. Whenever you find you are growing careless about prayer and careless about God's Word, then you will find you are losing faith, and so are losing power to overcome sin and to do the works of God. Oh! get back then as quickly as you can to your praying-place, and back to the Word of Life. Keep the band of faith firm and tight and you will never fail and never fall—for there is God's Word, a Word for living and a Word for dying—the gospel of Christ is the power of God unto salvation to every one that *believeth*.

XXIX

A TALK ABOUT TONGUES

THERE was a Greek prince long ago who wanted to give a splendid feast to his friends, and so he commanded his chief slave to provide a banquet of the best things that could be obtained, no matter what the cost was. When the guests arrived and the feast was spread, how astonished the prince was to find tongues, tongues, nothing but tongues! "Why is this?" he asked the slave. "Did not I order you to provide the best that could be found?" "And haven't I done it?" answered the slave; "for what is better than the tongue? With it we sing praises, with it we pray, with it we encourage and comfort one another—what is there in all the world better than the tongue?" The prince let it pass, but determined to try the cleverness of his slave in another way. So he ordered him to provide a feast of the worst things he could find. To his amazement, there was nothing at that feast either but tongues, tongues! "Why have you provided what was best," he asked, "when I ordered you to provide what was worst?" "And have I not done it?" asked the slave; "for what is worse than the tongue? With it men swear, and deceive, and cheat, and discourage, and wrong one another. What is there in all the world worse than the tongue?" That slave had evidently been thinking out things for himself, and had come to the conclusion that the tongue was the best or the worst thing we could have—just as we made use of it. And wasn't he right?

God gave us two eyes, but only one tongue, so telling us plainly that we should not talk about half that we see; and He gave us two ears, but only one tongue, telling us plainly we should not repeat one-half that we hear. And He has put our tongue inside our teeth, and made our lips also to close upon these, telling us plainly that our words must not leap out just as they like, but must be kept indoors till they are fit and proper to step outside.

It isn't every word that is to be trusted to go about as it likes. "Idle words" never should be. You know that "Satan finds some mischief still for idle *hands* to do;" and he is sure to find quite as much mischief for idle words, for "evil is wrought from want of thought, as well as want of heart;" so we need to take thought about our words, or they will be sure to do evil.

Who are the people who do most mischief in the place? They are the idle people. They have nothing particular to do, and so they go loafing about, shying at this thing, and breaking that, and spoiling the next.

It is the same with idle words. Since they have got nothing particular to do, they are not very particular about what they do, and so, without intending it perhaps, they do a great deal of evil.

Don't keep idle words about you, children. Give them something to do. When you send out your words, see that they have some errand to run, and that they have the right address to go to; see, that is, that they mean business, and that the business is good. Remember that not one word we utter is ever lost. It is a seed planted somewhere. If it is a good seed it will grow, and by-and-by the wind will blow its seeds to other fields, and somebody will be better for them. Idle words need not be dull words. The jest, the laugh, the merry quip are all good. They make sunshine, and sunshine brightens everything. All your life, as much as you can, speak sunshine: there are shadows and sorrows enough in the world; try to chase these away.

If nobody else remembers what we say, the angels do. Jesus once told His disciples something they could not understand. If you had been there, you could not have seen anybody but Jesus and His disciples. But after a time Jesus died, and when, in the cold grey morning, the women went to His grave, they saw two shining angels; and what did the angels say to them? They told them to remember the words that Jesus had spoken to His disciples. How did the angels know these words? Because they heard them when they were spoken. They were there with Jesus and the disciples; though you could not have seen them, they were there, listening, hearing, and they remembered what was said.

Think of that, and it will help you to think before you speak. Think of the angels, who are always hearing us, and remembering what we say, and who will put us in mind again of every word we have spoken. Think of that, and have nothing to do with idle words. Have a purpose for every one; and let that purpose be a good one, so that when the angels tell us again of what we said, we may listen with gladness and not with fear.

XXX

ANSWERS TO PRAYERS

"And all the devils besought Him, saying, Send us into the swine."
"And they began to pray Him to depart out of their coasts."
"He . . . prayed Him that he might be with Him."
—MARK v. 12, 17, 18.

HERE are three prayers, one of them good and two of them bad. Maybe they will teach us something. The disciples were good men who wished to be better, so they came to Jesus and asked, "Lord, teach us to pray." They had to learn how to pray aright, and had to learn from the best of all teachers—from Jesus Himself. So should we: there are things we need to be wise about if we would pray properly, and these three prayers may help us to this.

Here is what brought the three prayers together. Jesus had just crossed the stormy lake to save one soul. Yes, He went all that way, and took all that trouble, to save just *one*. How precious every soul must be to Him when He counts nothing a labour if it can only be saved! This was a poor man who was like a madman, he was so wild and wicked; all manner of evil spirits had taken possession of his heart. Ah!

there are people still who have unclean, very unclean spirits dwelling in them : all their thoughts are filthy, and all their doings are vile. Everybody turned away in fear from this man, but it was just because he was so bad that Jesus sought for him now. It is always His way; as doctors go where the sick are, to make them better, Jesus goes where the sinful are, to save them if they will let Him.

The devils that were in this poor man trembled when they saw Jesus. They knew Him: they had seen Him in heaven before He came to earth, and now they were afraid of Him—afraid that He would cast them out from their dwelling in this man's heart, and would leave them homeless, to shudder and drift in the winds. So they prayed: yes, the devils *prayed!*—but what a prayer! It was that they might be allowed to go into some swine that were near, and wallow with them. *Their prayer was granted!*—and they and the swine both soon came to a bad end. It was a prayer they should never have made.

The people who owned the swine were greatly troubled at their loss. But they were in an awkward fix; if they summoned Jesus before the magistrate, to make Him pay for the loss of the swine, they would be punished themselves, for they were Jews, and it was against the law for them to keep swine. They had been breaking the law all along, so they could not now ask the help of the law. But they were determined to stick to their sin and their swine, so—what do you think?—they also *prayed!* Yes, but what a prayer!—it was to ask Jesus to go away from them and never come back! They would rather have their sin than their Saviour! And their prayer also was answered: Jesus went away, and never returned. Could you bear that thought?—that Jesus had gone away from you, and taken His Holy Spirit with Him, and had abandoned you to your sins? Then take care how you want Him to keep out of the way that you may get doing the thing that is wrong. The worst thing we can do is to pray Jesus to leave us, because we prefer our sins, and the worst thing that can happen to us is to have that prayer answered.

But the third prayer is perhaps the strangest of all. It was the prayer of the man from whom the evil spirits had been cast out; he was now healed and in his right mind, and his heart was full of gratitude and love to Jesus. His prayer was a very beautiful and loving one: it was that he might go with Jesus and be with Him wherever He went. *But that prayer was refused!* He was told to stay where he was; he would do most good there, by telling others what Jesus had done for him. Two bad prayers were answered, while a good one was denied.

Is this puzzling? I don't think it should be: I think it should be very comforting and helpful to us. It should teach us this—should it not?—that sometimes Jesus is most loving when He does *not* answer our prayers. We are inclined to think hard thoughts of Him then—when He does not let us have our own way, or give us the things we want—yet see how it was here. Those who wanted to be worse, and to wallow more and more in sin, and those who were selfish, and preferred their gains to their God—they got what they wanted, because their hearts were dead-set on it; yet the granting of their wishes only brought sorrow on sorrow and loss upon loss on them at the last. Ah, children! when we are bent on a thing, and are determined to have it or to do it, it is not true prayer we are saying then, whatever words we may use, for true prayer always says to Jesus, "Grant this, please, if it is good for me, and good for others, and if it is what will please Thee; if not, then please do not answer it: Thou knowest best." This is true prayer, and the kindest, most merciful thing Jesus can sometimes do is *not* to let us have what we want.

It was for judgment He answered the two bad prayers, but it was in love He denied the prayer that was good. This man was saved, and if he remained where he was, and did what Jesus told him, you may be very sure it was that somebody else would be saved by him. Jesus needed him to be a missionary at home, instead of abroad, and so did not answer his prayer to go with Him, but left him where he was—and left him in love. By-and-by they would meet again in the glory, and there, maybe, there would also be those who were saved by this man,

Learn the lesson, then; don't be disappointed when your prayers are not answered as you would wish. Just think—it is the best prayer that is sometimes denied, and denied in tenderest love; and they are the worst prayers that are sometimes answered, but are answered in judgment and anger. Then leave it all with Jesus; tell Him what you would like to be or to do, but leave it with Him to decide what shall be best. So—just as the ship is steered by the helm—all your life will be guided by Jesus Himself, and when He guides, nobody misses God's blessing here, or His home in heaven at the last :—

> "Ill that He blesses is our good,
>   And unblest good is ill ;
> And all is right that seems most wrong,
>   If it be His sweet will."

XXXI

SWEETER THAN HONEY

"The law of kindness."—PROV. xxxi. 26.

SOME people make such queer use of the Bible! I have read of an old Scotch squatter in New South Wales who was taken dangerously ill. The minister—who lived far away in the nearest township—was sent for, but by the time he arrived the old man had mended so much that the minister found him seated on the verandah, not only reading the Bible, but evidently studying it with care, for he was taking notes from it. "I am glad," said the minister, "to see you so well employed." "Yes," replied the old man; "I've just been totting up the number of Job's sheep and mine, and I find that I have five thousand more than he had!" And that was all the use he was making of the Bible!

There are some people—especially ladies—who make no better use of this chapter. Because there are thirty-one verses in it—as many verses as there are days in a full-grown month—they make the chapter become a kind of almanac, and search it to see what it has to say for the day of the month on which they were born; they use the verses, in fact, as birthday mottoes! But there!—I see you are all wanting to do the same! Perhaps I shouldn't have told you! But if you only act up to the motto, you'll find it will be all right. Our particular text, however, is not for any one birthday; it is for every day, and for all the days of our life—the law of kindness in our tongues. That is something sweeter than honey.

Do you know what a "law" means? It is something that must be done, simply because it is right to do it. As long as we do it because we must, and not because it is right and good, it hasn't yet got right into our hearts. Just think of anybody saying to a good, kind, loving man, "You don't need to be kind any longer; we have changed the law; there is nothing now to compel you to be good!" How wonderingly the good man would look at him! "Why," he would say, "it doesn't matter to me whether you have changed the law or not. I didn't do good or love people because I was compelled; I did it simply because it was good to do it—it was right. Kindness is a law of itself, and that is enough for me." It is enough. If ever we would have the law of kindness on our lips, we must begin by having it in our hearts; we must love to do what is good and kind, simply because it is right, and not because we are compelled. It is RIGHT: that is the law, and it is enough.

But if we would get this sweetness into our hearts,

we must begin by *getting rid of thinking of ourselves first*. "Me first! me first!"—isn't that what some children say, and many more think, when there is anything nice to be had? Shame! shame! This is selfishness, and selfishness and kindness can never dwell together in the same heart. In the autumn of 1894, when the African royal mail steamer *Angola* was on the voyage from Madeira to Liverpool, a thrilling incident happened. Two men who were painting the outside of the vessel somehow both fell overboard. Captain Goudie at once put the ship about, and had the lifeboat lowered. As the boat at length came near one of the men struggling in the water he lifted his hand, and pointing to his comrade, who was almost exhausted, cried, "Save Bowman first! save Bowman first!" The boat turned aside and went to the other man and rescued him, and then went back and happily rescued the brave, unselfish fellow too. Wasn't he noble? Wasn't the law of kindness in his tongue? But mustn't it first of all have been in his heart for him in a time like this to think of his comrade before himself? And will *you* say, "Me first! me first!" Shame! shame!

Kindness and courage always go together: the bravest have always been the most thoughtful for other people. You all know the story of Sir Philip Sidney and his kindness to the poor dying soldier, but perhaps you do not know so well about Sir Ralph Abercrombie—as brave a man as ever lived. He was mortally wounded in the battle of Aboukir, and was carried on board the *Foudroyant*. To ease his pain a little a blanket was put under his head. He asked what it was. "Only a soldier's blanket," was the reply. "Whose blanket is it?" he inquired. "Only one of the men's." "I want to know his name," persisted the commander. "It is Duncan Roy, of the 42nd, Sir Ralph." "Then," said the brave man, closing his eyes for their last sleep, "see that Duncan Roy gets his blanket this very night." Even in a time like that the man who never feared shot or shell could think of the needs of a poor private soldier. And will *you* say, "Me first!" Shame! shame!

To be strong is to be kind, and kindness itself is stronger than all things else. Do you remember the story of the wind and the sunshine, trying which was stronger? The wind blew and blew its utmost, but the traveller only drew his cloak more firmly around him. But when the sunshine came, warm and soft, upon him, he unbuttoned his cloak and took it off. The gentle sunshine had done what the blustering winds could not do. And that is the power of kindness: it will do what nothing else can accomplish. One evening a young lady turning a street corner sharply, ran against a little, freckled, ragged boy, and you know how these boys can "speak up" when any accident like this happens. The lady stopped and turned to the boy with a smile, and said, "I beg your pardon. Indeed I am very sorry." The boy looked amazed for a second; then, taking off three-quarters of a cap—all he had—he bowed politely as he said, with a smile brightening up all his freckles, "You can have my parding, Miss, and welcome, and yer may run agin' me an' knock me clean down, an' I won't say a word!" After the young lady had passed he turned to a chum and said, as a kind of apology for being so unusually polite, "I never had any one ask my parding before, an' it kind o' took me off my feet." The sunshine, you see, was stronger than the gruff wind.

Did you ever hear about the whistling minister? Oh! he was a very famous man, and this is how he got his strange name. His church was in a very rough neighbourhood, where people didn't care for religion, and consequently he had a mere handful for a congregation. One day, when he was out walking in a quiet place, he came across a bright-faced little fellow of about five, and the two soon became friends, for the minister was very fond of children. He happened to mention how he nearly lost his dog, but got him again by whistling for him. The little fellow said he couldn't whistle. "Can't whistle!" said the minister. "How's that?" "'Cause nobody has had time to teach me," said the mite sadly. "Come along," said the kind-hearted man; "I'll teach you;" and taking the little fellow on his knee, puckering up their lips, the two were soon lost in their lesson. The two, in fact, became so engrossed in their task that they never noticed how a little crowd had gathered round them. That crowd made up its mind from that day about the new parson, that he was a real good fellow, and his church filled, and filled to the door. He was called "the whistling parson," and he was proud of his name, for it had done more than anything else to win the hearts of the people to him and to the message he had to teach them. It was but a little deed of kindness, but how strong it was!

Never think that kindness is lost. It never is. Not long ago a curious box was dug out of the ruins of Pompeii. It was made of marble or alabaster, about two inches square, and closely sealed. When opened it was found to be full of sweet perfume, like the fragrance of roses. For hundreds of years it had lain there, yet it was now as sweet as ever. It is always so with kindness; once done its sweetness never perishes. There was an alabaster box of ointment once broken, you remember, to anoint the Saviour, and He said the kindness would never, never be forgotten; and it has not been forgotten; we remember it now, and its sweetness has gone out into the world, and the world to-day is made the better for it. No! kindness is never lost.

The South Sea Islanders have a curious word for Hope. They call it *manaolana*, which means "the swimming thought." Hope, they say, is Faith swimming and keeping her head above water. That's a fine idea, but it won't do for kindness. It must be something more than a swimming thought. With some people it is never anything more; they have fine thoughts, fine fancies, always floating in their heads, but nobody is anything the better for them. They never *do* any good; they don't put the thought into practice. Kindness, true kindness, is very "worky"; it is always saying or doing something to make other people better or happier. It is only as it is kept working it is kept alive at all. There is an old legend that tells us how Thomas the Doubter, years after Christ had died and risen again, was very unhappy and had no peace. He went to the apostles and began to pour out his troubles in their ears, and they said they were very sorry, but they were so busy they really hadn't time to listen to him. Then he went with his complainings to some devout women, but they were as busy as Dorcas, and had no leisure to listen either. At last it occurred to him that perhaps it was just because they were all so busy that they were all so happy, while he was miserable only thinking about happiness and the want of it. So he took the hint, and went to Parthia, and preached the gospel there, and tried to do good to others whenever he got the chance; then the song of peace came into his heart again.

This is God's hint for us all: if we would be happy ourselves we must be always seeking to make others happy; if we would have the law of kindness in our tongues we must first have it in our hearts; but we mustn't keep it merely floating there, we must set it to work, for it is only as it is kept working it is kept living.

And you must not be discouraged because you often fail at first. The habit of kindness has to be learnt by little and little, and sometimes those who have been slowest at the start have been best in the end. Two boys—Arthur and William—were in the same school. The master, Mr. Rawson, said that Arthur was the stupidest boy he ever had, except William, who never seemed able to learn simple addition, let alone multiplication. Yet what do you think these two boys turned out to be? Arthur became Dean Stanley—one of the wisest and best of men—and William became the Prime Minister of England, and one of the cleverest arithmeticians in the land! They hadn't the gifts at the first, but they knew how to get them—by keeping on working at them, and so they got them, and got them greatly. So do not be discouraged if you are not always as kind and loving at the first as you would like and should be; try again, and again; keep at it, and it will come to be the habit of your life—the law of kindness will be always in your tongue, just because the love of kindness will be always in your heart.

But for this purpose you will need to keep the Kind One, Jesus, always before your mind. The great musician Gounod used to say, "When I was young I spoke always of myself alone. After a few years I condescended to add the name of Mozart, and say, 'I and Mozart.' But after I had studied and learnt a little more I thought I had better say, 'Mozart and I.' Now all I say is 'Mozart.'" That's the too common way. We begin by thinking a great deal of ourselves; then, perhaps, we think a little of Jesus also. But by-and-by, as we learn more, think more, and grow wiser, we think more and more of Jesus, till at last, as we come to know Him, and know ourselves better, we think and speak of Him only; for we have learnt that there is nothing kind, nothing right or good that we can do, but we need His help, and without that help we cannot do it. Then, if we would be wise, let us begin where we have all to end—by trusting Jesus, loving Him, praying to Him, making Him our example and our Saviour; so the law of kindness will be in our tongues, our hands, and our hearts, for it will be Jesus Himself who will be working through us.

XXXII

DRY STICKS

"Lay my staff upon the face of the child."—2 KINGS iv. 29.

IT was this way: a sad, sad mother came to the prophet Elisha, and wanted him to help her. Her little boy was dead, and she had only the one child. She could not give him up—could not let Death take him away; so she went to God's prophet, and asked him to come and bring her child to life again.

And Elisha was sorry for her, very sorry. He was a good and a kind man, and he wanted to help her. But he was very busy just then; he had a lot of other things to attend to, so he thought of a way that might do—he would send his servant with his staff, and if he laid the staff on the face of the child, that would be enough; it would bring the boy back to life again!

But it didn't; the staff was laid on the child's face, but the boy never opened his eyes, nor breathed nor stirred. And why?

First, because Gehazi, the servant, was a bad man. Yes, he was a cheat and a story-teller, and greedy; and though a bad man may do a great many things that good men do, he can never put *life* into any one. There is only one way of really doing good, and that is by being good yourself.

But next, the prophet himself had to learn a lesson. It was this: if ever you would do good to others, you must do it yourself. Some people are very busy all their days, but yet never do any good, because they don't try to do it themselves; they are always sending some dry stick or other to do it for them; they are always getting somebody else to do what God meant *them* to do. Do not you be of that spirit. Whenever you have a chance to do good, don't go about asking somebody else to do it for you. If God had meant this dry stick to raise the dead, He would have led the woman to pray to it. But she didn't ask the stick; she asked the prophet, because God meant the prophet himself to do this thing. And when God puts an opportunity before you of doing good, He means that you *can* do it if you will try; *you* can, but nobody else can, and that is why He gives you the chance of doing it.

Then do it, and do it yourself, and do it in love. When the staff failed the prophet had to go himself. How lovingly he did his work! He had learnt the lesson God meant to teach him. First, he asked to be left alone with the dead child. Ah! that is a great thing: if anybody has gone wrong, and you would put him right, if anybody has been naughty and you would do him good, then begin with him *alone.* Don't talk about the thing when others are present. Watch for a chance when you can have a quiet talk alone.

Then what did the prophet do? He "prayed unto the Lord." You must do the same. It is only from God we can get the power to do good; and if we forget to pray to Him, and trust in Him, and get help from Him, we may try, and try, but do no more good than the staff could do. You and the one you would do good to, *alone*, and then a bit of prayer— that is the way.

And then what did Elisha do? He cast himself down on the dead child, "and put his mouth upon his mouth"—think of that! warm, loving lips, pressed against cold, dead ones!—"and his eyes upon his eyes"—the eyes that could see on the eyes that could not—"and his hands upon his hands"—the hands that were warm and strong on the hands that were cold and weak; and so he brought the dead child back to life again. That was sympathy, the closest sympathy; and you never can do any real good to anybody till you have sympathy with him. A stick has no sympathy; neither has a coin, nor a crust. There is a use for these things in their own place, but there is no real good done except where there is love—the love that is willing to warm what is cold with its own heat—the love that brings its own life into contact with the dead—the love that prays, but also works—the love that has faith, but yet that does something too, as if everything depended on itself.

And love conquered; yes, love conquered even death, and the dead child was made alive again. Oh, what rejoicing there was that day! The mother rejoiced, and the prophet rejoiced, and God rejoiced too—rejoiced to see how all things had been done right, and death had been defeated.

Would you know something about that gladness? Then keep love uppermost, and whenever you get a chance to do good, set about it yourself; don't leave it to others to do. Get alone with the one you would do good to, have a word of prayer, and then show sympathy, and you will succeed; yes, you will succeed, for it is God Himself, Who never fails, Who will be working by you.

XXXIII

CROWN RIGHTS

"As we have, therefore, opportunity, let us do good unto all."—GAL. vi. 10.

THERE are some things you can back out of. If you have promised to do a thing, but haven't quite understood all about it, and afterwards you find it is wrong, then you can back out. There is nobody, and there is nothing in all the world, that can compel you to do wrong. It may need courage, it may bring much trouble with it, but sometimes the bravest thing that a boy or a girl, a man or a woman, can do is—to back out.

But there is one thing none of us has ever a right to back out of, and that is—doing good. We are as bound to do good, if we are going to live our lives rightly at all, as a star is bound to shine. We were made for it, we were sent into the world for it, and the fact that God has sent a new day to us is the surest sign we can have that He expects us to "do good." He wouldn't give us the new day, and send us fresh life, if He expected we would use it to do evil, would

He? Then make up your minds about this—that whatever else you have a right to do, or a right not to do, you have a right, the best of all rights—the right from God—to do good.

Here and there, as you go up and down the world, you see a notice stuck on some gate—"No admission except on business." You will never find a notice of that kind forbidding you from any chance you may have of doing good. The fact that there is a chance, and you want to take it, *is* business—good business, too—and you have a right to enter. The gates of this world had long been closed when, one starry night, a little Stranger opened and entered. His name was Jesus, and He grew to a man, and was loving through all, and His whole history has been condensed into these few words: "He went about doing good." Oh! if that could be put on our tombstone, and be truthfully put, we could not have a grander epitaph. If you passed along and read on the monument of this great soldier that he conquered in such-and-such battles, and on the monument of that great king that he ruled over so many nations, and on that of the rich man that he owned such-and-such broad estates, you might admire and wonder; but when you came to a modest little stone, which simply said, "He went about doing good," you would say, "This was the best and noblest of them all." Look ahead of you, then, children; there is a stone lying somewhere or other now that shall be chiselled one day with your name upon it. May that day be far off, for the sake of all the good that you can do between this and then; but it comes; live so that you will, at all events, deserve to have put on it the words, "He went about doing good."

Notice, then, to whom the good is to be done. It is to all. All? Yes, all! I know that is where the hard part comes in. It is not so difficult to do good to the good; not so hard to be kind to the kind, and pleasant to the pleasant, and loving to the loving. My dog can do all that; but if I am to be something better than my dog I must do more—I must school my heart and train my spirit to do good to the disagreeable, the unpleasant, and the people who don't care a straw for me, or perhaps dislike me very much. Yes, all!

And why? Just because the worse they are, the more they need all the good I can do them. If you saw a poor horse hurt itself—kicking the shafts, tearing its mouth on the bit, and grazing its knees with wild stumbling on the stones—would you whip it? would you be angry with it? A man who understands horses would not; he knows that the poor thing has got a wrong idea somehow into its head, and he would stroke it and pat it, and speak soothingly to it, till he had won its confidence again. He would do it good, just because that was what it most needed then. And it is the same with people: they get wrong ideas into their heads about you, or about somebody else, or about something else, and then they go wrong. Is that any reason why you should go wrong too? Isn't it rather the reason why you should do good, and be good, and so help those who are wrong or wicked to get right again?

Yes, all!—for that is God's way. He sees all the evil that is done in the world, but He is so patient! He sends the sunshine and the rain on the evil as well as the good, in the hope that His kindness will yet touch their hearts and bring them all to Him. He is so patient, so loving! And what your business, and mine, in the world must be is to be like Him. So don't pick and choose those to whom you should do good. There are your orders—"Do good to all!"

But when? When you have paid them back for any evil they have done? When you "have had it out" with them and got the victory? No, not then; it is then generally too late. The exact time is fixed for us here according to God's great clock. Here it is—"As we have opportunity." When the chance comes, then is our time, and it is all we have to consider. Now, when can you get a better chance for doing good than when some one else is doing evil? To do good when people are doing good is very nice, and always helps to make things nicer; but to do good when people are doing evil is better, for it is double good; it helps to stop the evil from going farther on the one hand, and, on the other, it plants a seed that will thrive and grow; for God's angels always watch over, and water, and bring to fruit every good thing that is done. A great many things have to be advertised for because they are lost, but never a good deed—that is never lost. Some way, somehow, somewhere, it is always found again with its fruit upon it.

Then watch for your chance: that's all. It is God's chance for you. When it comes do good; you have nothing more to consider. God will take care of all the rest. But see that you do watch for your chance. There is such a thing as looking the other way when the chance is coming along, and then, of course, you don't see it. That is what you try to say to yourself, but God says something different. He says, "You *would not* see it!" What happens then? Just this: it is written down that you did evil when you had the opportunity of doing good, for to have the chance and not to take it is sin.

But one little word more upon this text. It is this—take it all home to yourself. It says, "Let *us*," and I am always a bit afraid of that "us." When we say *us*, or *we*, or *ours*, we are very apt to take it to mean anybody or everybody *but* ourselves. If we would do good then, we must begin by reading the text in this way: "As I have opportunity, let me do good unto all." Resolve upon this, make it the one grand purpose of your life, for the love of Jesus, Who loved us even to death, and you will never miss the way to heaven, for every deed of kindness, every word of help or pity, will be another and another footprint of the Saviour to guide you on, for you will then be a follower of Him Who "went through the world doing good."

XXXIV

"*BRAKES DOWN!*"

"Slow to speak."—JAMES i. 19.

THERE is a great difference between being slow to speak and being a slow speaker. A slow speaker gives me the fidgets; I want to put a pin into him to hurry him up a bit! Perhaps it's because I am a quick speaker myself—more's the pity, very often!—but yet it's awful to hear any one drawling his words as if he had a thousand years and a day longer to say all he wanted to say! To be "slow to speak" means—Don't be in a hurry to talk, but when you have to do it, reel it off as smartly as you can.

What is the swiftest thing in the world? Ah, you may well say, "Ask me another—and an easier one!" There is the greyhound; how it slips along—swift and soft as a shadow! And there is the racehorse—gone like a flash! And there is the lightning: it is here, there, everywhere, before you have quite made up your mind where it is. These are all swift—and every one swifter than another—but none of them is the swiftest.

Do you give it up? Shall I tell you—the swiftest thing in the world? It is *thought*. Yes; with most people there is nothing so rapid as that—nothing! There is the sea, for example, with its rolling waves and the *sh*, *sh*, *sh* of the pebbles on the beach when the billow goes back. You are thinking of that now—and yet the sea is fifty miles off, if it is a yard. And there are the stars; how they flash and glitter on a clear frosty night!—God's lamps set twinkling in the dark to cheer us on. You are thinking of them now, yet between the sea and the stars there are sometimes millions of miles. But it has taken you only half a minute to think of the one and the other! What a distance your thoughts have travelled in that time! The lightning couldn't do it; it would have to come panting up long, long after your thought had sat down and got a rest.

Yes, as I said, with most people *thought* is the swiftest thing in the world. But it is not so with everybody. There are some people who have something that is swifter than thoughts. They are their *words*. Yes, their words are very, very swift—so swift, indeed, that they often speak before they think! Their words are out, are off and away, and do their mischief, and then their thoughts come along, covered with perspiration, to tell them they have made a mistake—but it is too late. The harm is done; the words had got too great a start of the thoughts.

Let me tell you a case of the kind—one that touched

me very much when I read it. It was in America, where people sometimes travel great distances in trains that have sleeping-carriages, which they call "cars." Here is the story:—

"One night, in a crowded sleeping-car, a baby cried most piteously. At length a harsh voice called out from a neighbouring berth, 'Won't that child's mother stop its noise, so that the people in this car can get some sleep?' The baby ceased for a moment, and then a man's voice answered, 'The baby's mother is in her coffin in the baggage-car, and I have been awake with the little one for three nights; I will do my best to keep her quiet.' There was a sudden rush from the other berth, and a rough voice, broken and tender, said, 'I didn't understand, sir; I am so sorry; I wouldn't have said it for the world, if I had understood. Let me take the baby and you get some rest;' and up and down the car paced the strong man, softly hushing the tired baby until it fell asleep, when he laid it down in his own berth and watched over it till morning. As he carried the little one back to its father, he again apologised in the same words: 'I hope you will excuse what I said; I didn't understand how it was.'"

No, he hadn't understood: his words had gone ahead of his thoughts, and when his thoughts came up and showed him what a cruel mistake he had made he was sorry, sorry, the good-hearted man. For he was good-hearted; only, he hadn't learnt to be "slow to speak."

We must try to be better; to think first and speak

next—to put the horse before the cart,, and not the cart before the horse; thoughts before words, and not words before thoughts. We shall never be sorry for doing this, but, oh! we shall often be sorry, sorry if we speak first and think afterwards.

But how are we to be "slow to speak" when we are excited, or angry, or cross? Well, the old rule used to be that when you were angry you should count fifty before you spoke. That is perhaps a very good rule for some people, but it never did for me. I have tried it. Oh yes!—when my temper was up and my heart was thump, thump, thumping, I have said to myself, "One, two, three, four, five, six," and so on, and I have kept fairly well at it till I came to ten or fifteen, and then I always found that somehow I began to count by fives or by tens—"fifteen, twenty, thirty, forty, *fifty!*"—and then the words I had been bottling up would fly out, and drench the other person, as I had meant they should do!

But by-and-by—when I had time to think—when my thoughts came weary-footed behind my words—then I have often felt so sorry and ashamed, and wished I had learnt to be "slow to speak!" But counting has never helped me, and—between ourselves—I don't think it has ever helped anybody.

There *is* a surer way and a better one: it is simply this—*think of Jesus.* That's all—a little thought of Him—thinking He is there and wondering what He would say, or what He would do—that's enough! It makes you hold your tongue till a bit of a prayer has gone up from your heart, and that makes everything look so different. You feel kinder then, gentler, a little more patient, and that makes you "slow to speak," but so swift to help and swift to think the best, rather than the worst, of others.

So, children (to put all I have to say about this text into a word), whenever you feel tempted to be hasty rather than slow to speak, think of Jesus, and do only what He would have you do, say only what He would have you say, and you will never regret it.

XXXV

BIG-HEARTED

"Who is my neighbour?"—LUKE x. 29.

NOT a very difficult question to answer, you would think. Why, he had only to go next door and inquire, if he wanted to know! Yes, but we have more neighbours than those who dwell near us; only nobody thought of this till Jesus came and taught us. Before then people asked—not, "Who is my neighbour?" but, "Who *isn't* my neighbour? Whom am I *not* obliged to be kind to? Whom may I pass by and care nothing about?" They did not want to find out whom they should love and help, but rather to find out whom they were not *obliged* to love. As if you could love anybody because you were obliged! Why, the moment you say to love, or to sympathy, or to charity, "You are *obliged* to do it," it ceases to be love or sympathy or charity, and becomes duty and taxes—duty and taxes only.

Do not get this kind of religion into your heart. There is a good deal of it about, so you must watch against infection. There are people, that is, who are always asking, "*Must* I do this for Christ's sake? *Must* I do that?" They are always wanting to discover what is the *least* they can do to be saved. That is not love's way; love's way is to find out what is the *most* it can do, and it does not wait to be obliged at all; it simply does it because it will please the Lord. That is the right religion—the religion which asks—not, "Who isn't my neighbour?" but "Who is?—who is the one I can help and be kind to?"

And Jesus tells us: He says it isn't the person next door, just because he is next door, or the person in the next street, because he happens to be in the next street; it is that person anywhere in all the world who needs our help, and to whom we can give it. Remember this. If there is a poor, sickly, suffering child anywhere, and you can do anything to make things easier or better for that child, then that one is your neighbour, and you must show yourself neighbourly to him by doing all you can just for Christ's sake.

This is the way to grow the big, kind heart; the other is the way to grow the little and the mean one. Be big-hearted; do not ask, "What is the least I can do to show my love for Jesus?" but, "What is the most?" Not, "Am I obliged to help?" but "Have I a chance to help?" If you have, then take it—that's the way to grow like Jesus.

XXXVI

MULTUM IN PARVO

"Even a child is known by his doings."—PROV. xx. 11.

"EVEN a child!" What a way of speaking!—as if a child were of no importance! You don't think so—and I don't think so—and Solomon didn't think so; it was only his way of putting it. What he means to say is this—for all that a child is so little, you can tell what kind of a man or woman he or she will grow up to be.

It is said you may know a tree by its fruit. That is so; but it is only one way of knowing it. You can tell it by its leaf as well as by its fruit, for every tree has its own kind of leaf—the oak has one sort, the chestnut another, and the fir-tree another still.

You could even tell a tree by its bark, for every kind of tree has its own sort of bark. Or, if you were to cut out a bit from the tree, a good carpenter would guess very sharply the name of the tree the block came from. And even when the tree is only a little baby, an inch or two above the ground, if you were to cut a little bit off (though it could ill spare it!), yet there are people who would tell you what sort it was from that little specimen. But, more wonderful still, when it is only a seed there are wise men who could tell you for certain what kind of a tree would grow out of that seed once it was planted. You see, every bit of a tree tells what it is, when it is old and wrinkled, but also when it is young and smooth. And it is just the same with us; we are all of a piece, so that even a child can be known by his doings.

"It doesn't matter what I do now," I heard a boy say to another the other day; "it'll be different when I am a man." Oh! that is a big, big mistake. It is what you are now, and what you do now, that shows what you will be by-and-by.

A little Swedish boy tumbled out of a window and was hurt, but he would not cry. The king, Gustavus Adolphus, said, "That boy will make a man to be depended on in an emergency." And he did; he became the famous General Bauer.

A woman fell into a river in Italy, but though there was a crowd of men standing by, no one dared to jump in after her. But a little fellow did; he struck the water almost as soon as herself, and managed to keep her up till help came. Everybody said that the boy was very daring, very kind, very quick, but also very reckless, and so he showed himself to be when he was a man, for that boy was Garibaldi.

There was a little fellow who used to paint and draw very cleverly and very patiently. A famous old painter watched him for a little while, and then said, "That boy will beat me one day." And so he did, for he was Michael Angelo.

Even a child then, you see, is known by his doings. Never think it doesn't matter what you do now; it matters *everything*.

There was a rich man in Manchester who died some time ago—John Rylands, "the Wellington of commerce," as he was called. He lived to nearly ninety, and went to his business every day. One day, however, at the last, when his coachman drove him as usual to the grand building where his office was, he turned away peevishly, saying, "No, no! I want to go to my own place." His mind had gone back over sixty years to the little humble shop from which he had started. He had forgotten all about the great wealth and the grand buildings he had made since then; he was back again to the early beginning.

And why? Because it is what we learn and what we do when we are young that sticks longest and closest to us all our days. So, children, look to your doings now, if you would have them right and good and true when you grow up. Whatever you do, do it as if Jesus were with you. Get into the habit of thinking of Him, speaking to Him, consulting Him about everything. It is a habit you can learn, and it is the sweetest and best you ever will acquire. Look to Him and keep with Him, and you will never need to be ashamed of your doings. Nobody ever had a heartache yet for what he did to please Jesus.

XXXVII

PILOT WANTED!

"Made shipwreck."—1 TIM. i. 19.

THERE'S nothing sadder! To see the gallant ship clear out of the harbour, with all sail set and pennons flying—like a bright, strong youth going out to face the world—and then to see the same ship, when the storm is past and the sun has come forth again, lying broken among the rocks, a poor, crushed, bruised, battered thing—this is as sad a sight as we can ever see. I have seen it, seen it many times; seen it with ships and seen it with men and women, and it always makes the heart ache.

Let me tell you about a couple of shipwrecks that have something to teach us. There was the *Nepaul*, one of the finest vessels we had in our merchant fleet. A few years ago she set out from China, homeward bound, and passed in safety through all the dangers of the great broad seas she had to cover, till she had almost reached Devonport, her destination. But there was a thick fog hanging over the waters, and the captain's signals for a pilot could not be seen. He should have anchored then and waited. Ah! it's a great thing, children, to learn, when you have done all that you can do, to stand, simply stand, and wait for God to work. But the captain would not wait; he thought he knew the coast well enough to pilot his vessel himself into Devonport, and so he went on and on, making for the harbour, till suddenly there was a crash and a lurch, and the beautiful ship was a total wreck—a wreck almost within reach of the haven!

What was the captain's fault? *Presumption.* He would not wait for a pilot; he thought he knew as much of the coast as the men did who spent their lives in learning. And presumption is our great sin when we think we can get to heaven without the great Pilot, Jesus Christ. We can't do it; we may get very near; God may be very good and very patient with us, and protect us in many dangers, but no one can enter the Good Haven unless the flag of the Cross shows that Jesus has the command. Run up the flag now, my bairnies; let Jesus have the command of your life. When the pilot comes on board the captain steps down; he becomes then but the chief officer, who takes his instructions from the pilot. That's how it must be with us, if we would enter the Harbour at last, with full sail and happiness, to receive an "abundant" entrance. Don't trust to your own knowledge or your own cleverness; trust Jesus, "Jesus only," if you would avoid the shipwreck of your life. Do it at once; you can't tell the rocks you may have to steer through to-morrow.

The other wreck was just as sad.

The steamship *Central America*, on a voyage from New York to San Francisco, sprang a leak in mid-ocean. A vessel, noticing her signal of distress, bore down toward her. Seeing the danger to be very great, the captain of the rescue-ship spoke to the *Central America*: "What is amiss?"

"We are in bad repair, and going down; lie by till morning," was the answer.

"Let me take your passengers on board now."

But it was night, and the commander of the *Central America* did not like to send his passengers, for that would cost the price of their passage, and thinking the ship could be kept afloat a while longer, replied, "Lie by till morning."

Once more the captain of the rescue-ship cried, "You had better let me take them now."

"Lie by till morning," was sounded back through the trumpet.

About an hour and a half afterward her lights were missed, and though no sound had been heard, the *Central America* had gone down, and all on board perished, just because it had been thought they could be saved better at another time.

That is how most people are wrecked. It is by delay—by putting off and putting off to a more convenient season. Children, we have never any right to study our own convenience only: we need to study the convenience of others as well, or we shall soon be all wrong, and put others wrong too. Now, whatever time we may think convenient for us, there is only one time that is convenient for God. That time is *Now!* "*Now* is the accepted time: *Now* is the day of salvation." "Put off, put off!"—that is what Satan whispers. "Now, Now, NOW!"—that is what God is calling. Which voice will you obey? The Lord help you to decide for Christ *now*, so, over whatever seas you may have to sail, or through whatever storms you may have to pass, you will be "kept"—"kept by the power of God unto salvation ready to be revealed" when the fogs are lifted.

XXXVIII

THE KIND HEART

"Thou shalt not see thy brother's ox or his sheep go astray, and hide thyself from them; thou shalt in any case bring them again unto thy brother."—DEUT. xxii. 1.

LET me tell you one of the finest things I have heard of for a long time. A number of schoolboys were going home together, when, in a quiet street, they came upon an old broken-down cart, with an older and still more broken-down horse between the shafts. It was such a poor, weak, starved-looking thing! What do you think the boys did? Tease it? laugh at it? jeer at it? No; they did something better and grander than that: they clubbed their coppers among themselves, went off to the nearest corn-chandler's, and bought the horse a good feed of oats! How it munched! How it wagged its old ears! How it held up its head inches higher when the oats were finished! These were gentle boys: every one had the making of a Christian gentleman in him. They had the Kind Heart. When they saw the poor thing they didn't "hide" from it—did not, that is, pretend they hadn't noticed how weak and hungry it was: they saw what was wanted, and set to work themselves to do the best they could. Wasn't it a fine thing? If you had seen it you couldn't have helped saying, "God bless those lads!" Ay! and He would bless them, too,—as He always does bless the Kind Heart.

And it is all about the Kind Heart this text is speaking. What it says is,—If you find any dumb creature that has gone astray and got lost, and you know to whom it belongs, then don't pretend you haven't seen it, and so allow it to be lost. You *have* seen it: that is enough. Be ready to take a little trouble to restore it to its owner again. If it were your horse, or your dog, or your sheep that was lost, this is what you would like somebody to do for you. Then be ready—always ready—even though it puts you to a bit of trouble, to do for others what you would have others do for you.

But if we are told, as God's children, that this is what we must do for the poorest of poor dumb creatures, how much more must we be ready to do it for boys and girls and men and women? The poorest and saddest of these is worth millions more than all the oxen or sheep in the world. Yet they sometimes go astray: they go wrong, and they do wrong, and wander away from Jesus. Then when we find them, wherever they are; when we see what has gone wrong and how it has gone wrong, we mustn't "hide" ourselves—mustn't pretend we haven't seen. We *have* seen—Jesus knows it—and that is enough. We must now do all we can to put right what has gone wrong and bring back the wandering ones to God, Who is the great Owner of us all. This is what Jesus did for us. We had all wandered away from God, like lost sheep, and He saw our mistakes and our sins and our unhappiness, and He came to bring us back and save us. That was the Kind Heart: it is kindest of all in Jesus. But we must have it too if we belong to the Lord, and this is the way both to get it and show it—by thinking for others, caring for others and not for ourselves only, and by being always ready with a helping hand and a helping heart wherever and whenever they are needed.

XXXIX

INWARD RICHES

"Goodly pearls."—MATT. xiii. 45.

Do you like to hear about jewels and gems? I should think you did, by the hearty way you always sing the hymn—

"When He cometh, when He cometh,
To make up His jewels."

Let me speak, then, for a little about pearls. You know what they are like—little snowdrops, round and smooth. They cost a deal: you needn't expect to be able to buy one by saving up your school ha'pence. Cleopatra—you have heard of her?—swallowed a pearl of the value of £80,000! Think of that! It is all very well for one swallow to make a summer, but to swallow a fortune in this fashion is a luxury which only Eastern princesses, or people in story-books, can enjoy. It has been calculated that if Adam had been set to till the ground at fifteen shillings a week—the pay of many a day-labourer—and he had tried to save up, he wouldn't, up to the present time, have saved as much as the Queen gets in a year! And yet there are many people in the land far richer than the Queen. How long, then, do you think it would take you to save out of your school ha'pence enough to buy a pearl like Cleopatra's? Do you think I am going to tell you? Not very likely! In the first case I am not very good at figures; and in the next, this is such a tough sum that I think it had better be kept for an "imposition" task! Suggest it to your master, with my compliments.

Any way, we see that these pearls cost a deal; Cleopatra's was a mere trifle to some of them. There was one sold to the Shah of Persia for £180,000, and another once fetched £150,000. It's fine to think about such great sums, is it not?—makes you feel quite princely or princessly! But the banker's clerk, who tots up millions in the ledger, has to be content with a humble chop when he gets home, and we shall have to get along with our ha'pence, as best we may, in spite of all our familiarity with these great figures.

Yet, though it costs so much, how do you think the pearl is made? By real Christian gentleness! Yes! —that's all! It is in this way. When the oyster is quietly minding its own business and not interfering with anybody, some intruder comes upon it—a grain of sand, or bit of metal, or something of that kind— and the intruder won't go away again, but settles down, and makes up his mind to stay. What would you do in a case of that kind? I am afraid to think of what you would do; afraid to think of what I would do! But I like to think of what the oyster does, and I feel very much humbled before its better spirit. Instead of fretting, sulking, bemoaning its misfortune, or calling in the police, it quietly sets to work to change the misfortune into a blessing! It kills the intruder—but kills him with kindness. It gives him the very best it has got; it lays before him, and loads around him, the sweetest and finest dishes it can make, with the result that the intruder perishes, and the oyster, good, kind thing, is so sorry about this mishap that she straightway embalms the body, and gives it the costliest coffin she can make—and that is the pearl. Yes; the finest pearl, which costs thousands and thousands of pounds, is only the coffin which the kindly oyster made for something or other that was very impertinent and came where it wasn't wanted. You can test this for yourself. Cut open one of these pearls—the hundred-and-eighty-thousand-pound one will do—and at the heart of it you will find the intruder, better embalmed than Joseph was—and better than he deserved to be!

Can a little lowly shell-fish show a grand and loving spirit like this, and shall we fail to show a similar one? However humble our teacher may be, then, let us learn from the oyster the gracious art of turning evil into good, and making pearls of the very things that would otherwise do us harm. It is the only way in which we can grow up right, good, loving men and women.

Does anybody, for instance, do you an injury? Then, if you think of that injury, and of it only, it will rankle, and rankle, and fester, and fester in your mind till it makes the heart bitter and sour and evil. But forgive it: think that perhaps the injury was not meant after all, or that the one who did it was not aware of all that he was doing; bring a kind and loving thought to bear on it all, and at once the evil work is stopped, the bitterness departs, and you have made your own heart sweeter for the grace of pardon that has come into it. You have healed the wound with a "goodly pearl."

Have you heard something naughty and bad about some one? Don't let it get into your heart so as to make you think evil thoughts of the one who has been spoken against. Wait till you *know;* maybe the story is not true, or maybe it has been exaggerated. Believe the good till the evil is proved, and even then try to think of what provocation or temptation the other may have had, and remember that you yourself may be tempted. Do not take delight in the wrong-doings of others; try rather to cover them with a cloak of charity, as the oyster covers the thing that else would irritate with a coating of precious pearl. This is to be really loving and Christ-like, and by doing it your own soul will be richer.

It was so—was it not?—that Jesus made the cross itself become so precious to us all? At one time it was looked on as the most hateful and hideous thing in the world, but now it has become the best, the grandest, and most beautiful. Why? Because, even when He was on the cruel cross, Jesus prayed for those who were ill-treating Him, and all that He said and did there was loving and pitiful and kind. It was there —when men meant destruction—that Jesus brought in salvation—the salvation which has become for us all "the pearl of great price." May we all learn, then, the sweet and Christ-like art of praying for our enemies, and doing kindness to those who are unkind to us, and changing all injuries into pearls!

XL

MONKEY TRICKS

"Apes."—1 KINGS x. 22.

THESE were some of the curious creatures which Solomon's ships brought from afar. Maybe you don't admire his taste, and maybe you do, but monkeys are queer things any way. They are so like ourselves, and yet so unlike, that it makes one positively shy sometimes to look at a cageful of them—almost seems as if we were being introduced to our poor relations, who don't know how to behave themselves in good company! One of them was so human-like, through all his tricky ways, that an enthusiastic Irish priest, who had been watching him, so far forgot himself as to cry out, "Spake but a wurrd an' I'll baptize ye!"

There was a quaint old preacher who once said that Satan was God's ape! There was a good deal of shrewdness in the remark: it expressed very much. Whatever God does, Satan always mimics; he gets up an imitation somewhat like the original, and palms that off for the real thing, and a great many people—nations even—are certain to be duped by it.

Learned people speak about "original" sin; I suspect, however, when you come to look at it closely, you will find very little that is original about it. It is all the same old story—an attempt to make evil look like good, and pass off an imitation for the genuine article. There is not much that is original about it, in this sense at all events.

You children are sometimes called "young monkeys,"—but that is meant kindly, and is spoken with a smile, and you don't mind it. I do not think, however, you would like it so well if you were called apes. Yet—would you believe it?—not a few bright boys and girls come to be little else! The older they grow, and the higher they climb, the more of the monkey they show! See how.

There's Charlie: he's a great mimic—can "take off" almost anybody. Isn't he funny! and doesn't he make you laugh! Yes; and it is that laugh of yours that is spoiling the lad. He likes it, he lives for it, watches for every chance to draw it out, and so is always taking notice of people's weak points, their oddities and defects, that he may show them all up again before you and others, in order to draw out that laugh which is becoming the sweetest of perfumes to him. Poor Charlie! he doesn't know, doesn't think, that he is killing off all the best that is in him. But he is: he is taking the surest way of coming at length to be unable to see the good that is in people, and the things that are lovely and strong. There was an artist once—Breughel—who had so given himself to the painting of witches, and imps, and satyrs, and creatures of that sort only, that when at length he wanted to paint a portrait he could not do it. He was sure to make the face impish somehow—putting a leer into the eyes, or a sneer on the lips. By watching for these things too much he had come to be unable to see anything else. Poor Charlie is fairly on the way to do the same if he does not quickly stop his clever apishness, and set himself to copy, not the worst, but the best that is in other people.

And there is Tom: how his tail is growing! He began with smoking: he thought it made a man of him! What a caricature! Bad is the best in a case like this, but this is about the worst. Once you could see *Tom*—a bright-faced, promising lad as ever was—but now you can only see a big cigarette, with a little boy dragged at the end of it. If he only knew the figure he cuts! Unfortunately, the mirror that shows us our true selves has yet to be invented, and Tom goes on, dragged by suction, at the end of his cigarette. And now he is learning something more; he has got acquainted with Ben Raikes, the "knowing one," who is in the secret of all the racing-stables, and Tom can already give the wink, and talk turf, and invite the betting, even as Ben does. Poor Tom! there's good stuff in him, but he is going all wrong, for want of seeing the difference between imitating and aping.

It's the same with Bessie: she reads novels and

romances, and a great deal besides that is very good in its way, but what does she make of them all? Sham, gilding, veneer only! One day she is sweet and gentle—everything you could wish; but the next day she is as proud as Lucifer, and everything you don't like. The fact is, Bessie isn't there at all: there is only an ape—or apess, if that is the right gender—who is trying to live over again the characters that have taken her fancy in the latest novel she has been reading. It is a bit hard on her mother; when she wakes up in the morning the good woman never knows whether she has a princess for a daughter—a princess waiting for the prince to come along—or whether she has got a pirate's bride, who cuts off heads, and smashes things, and behaves strangely. Sometimes she is the one, sometimes the other, but never anything for long. It's different with her sister, Dora; she reads quite as much as Bessie does, but she sticks by her New Testament, and whatever squares with that in the books she reads she tries to imitate: the rest she happily forgets. The one is genuine, trying to be better, but the other is only aping.

Learn to imitate, but don't ape. Never try to raise a laugh at the expense of other people's feelings or failings. As you grow older you will find all the world of difference between being laughed *at* and laughed *with*. You only laugh *at* an ape, but you laugh *with* the good-hearted boy or girl who is making bright, genuine, but innocent fun. Imitate: don't ape. To imitate is to copy the best we see or read about, so as to make it a part of ourselves, and have it for our very own, everywhere and always, even when we are not thinking about it. But to ape!—this is to make mere clowns of ourselves, to amuse or sadden other people, and to pay for the privilege of doing so by parting with the best that is in us, and spoiling for ourselves the days that are yet to be, and the beautiful things that are to be seen in the world, and are to be found in everybody, if we will only seek them out, rather than seek for their failings and oddities. Be genuine, and imitate only that which you would yourself like to be when you grow up. Keep clear of the ape!

XLI

BIG AND LITTLE

"Some great thing."—2 KINGS v. 13.

I HEARD once of a poor half-witted fellow who was found shivering on a bitter, cold winter night on a lonely country road. The moon was shining very brightly, and it turned out that when the poor, half-witted lad saw the shadow of the parish church, so deep and dark before him, he had come to the conclusion that the brook had overflowed, and he was waiting there until the water had subsided, so that he might pass safely over. Hindered by a shadow from going on! Oh! there are many people like him, though you might hesitate to say they were half-witted.

If there is one shadow that does this more than another—that hinders us from doing the good in the world we might do, it is the ambition to do some *great* thing that is far off, before we will attempt to do some *good* thing that is very near, but may seem very little. Children, you must learn to face that shadow and force your way through it. When once we get into the way of thinking or speaking of things as great or little, we are as far out of our right calculations as if we had twisted the multiplication table upside-down and anyhow! There is nothing little with God, and nothing great. A dewdrop is as dear and as precious to Him as a great star. He rules and reigns over the whole world, and yet He looks after the sparrow's fall. As He judges of things so must we—not by their bulk, not by their glitter, but by whether they are doing the thing they were meant to do. The rivet isn't so great as the engine, but if the rivet gets loose the engine breaks down, and that shows that the thing we call little may be as important as the thing we call great.

Treasure it in your hearts then, children, that there is something every one of you can do for God. It is not for you to ask whether it is great or little, but only to ask whether it is the thing God would have you do for Him *then*. Oh, the glory of doing little things for Christ, and doing them lovingly and doing them well, just for His sake!

That was a fine thing I read about the other day. A policeman in Glasgow saw a poor woman pick up something from the street, quickly put it in her apron, and then hurry on. Thinking it was something valuable, he went up and asked her what it was she was concealing. The woman was very confused, and would not answer him for a time, and that, of course, only confirmed his suspicions. But at last she opened her apron, and what was there?—only a few pieces of broken glass. The important policeman felt, of course, a little crestfallen. Her explanation, however, was very touching. "I thought," she said, looking at the bits of broken glass, "that I would take them out of the way of the bairns' feet." You know in Scotland, in the summer-time, the children like to go about barefooted, and this dear, good woman, poor as she was, had a motherly heart, and removed out of the way of the children's feet what might have hurt them. "That was not a very great thing," some might say; but the angels would say it was one of the greatest, because it was done in the spirit of love. Don't you think, when you get the chance, you also might do something like this?

Couldn't you, too, do something or say something sometimes that might help and encourage another? Many years ago a gentleman was visiting a little village school in Ireland. One boy was very backward in his spelling. "I can make nothing of that lad," said the teacher; "he is the stupidest boy in the school." The gentleman was surprised at this, for the lad had a bright, intelligent face. Putting one of his hands on the little fellow's noble brow, he said, "One of these days you may be a fine scholar; don't give up; try, my boy, try!" The kind word and kind look roused the soul of the boy. From that day he applied himself diligently to his tasks, and afterwards came to be known throughout the world as the great preacher and scholar, Dr. Adam Clarke. Was it a little thing this gentleman did that day? Perhaps it was, but it was like a little seed that afterwards produced great fruit.

It was the end of the Dorcas for the season, and two young girls were busy making flannel dresses for the poor. "There," said one of them, laying down her work with a sigh of relief, "that is all that I need do for a while." "Wait just a minute more," said the other, and she went into another room, and came back with some skeins of silk and a few knots of ribbon and lace. "What are you doing?" her companion asked, as she saw her putting a dainty crimson edging here, a little frilling there, and fastening on the bright ribbons. "Why, it only takes a minute or two to do it," said the other, with a smile, "and I want to make the dress pretty for some mother's baby." Wasn't that a kind thing to do? And yet it seemed so little! But a great deal of good came from it. One poor mother sobbed when she received that dress. "Only to think," she said, "that any one cared so much for my baby!"

Make up your minds about it, children, that the little things may be the very greatest. Naaman the leper wanted to be healed, and the prophet told him to go and wash in the Jordan. That was such a simple thing to do, however, that he felt insulted. If the prophet had asked him to do something great or very difficult, then he might have supposed he would get healing; but simply to wash in the Jordan! —that seemed too little a thing for so great a man to do. And yet when he did it at last in simple faith, behold, he was healed!

It is just the same with our salvation. We are asked to believe on the Lord Jesus Christ; the promise is, that we shall then be saved. Is it a little thing to believe in Jesus? If it is, it is little as the seed is little, as the first beams of the dawn are little, as the first trickle of the fountain is little; by-and-by the little seed becomes a great tree, the little beams of the dawn become the glaring noontide light, and the little fountain becomes the broad, deep river. Do the little thing, then, if you would rejoice in the great one—which is our salvation. "Only believe," and the Lord will work with you to do all the rest.

But just because you believe on the Lord Jesus, you must show it by a loving, kindly, helpful spirit to others. Jesus went through the world doing good, and if we are His we must be followers in His footsteps. Don't wait, then, until you can do some great thing; rather try at once—to-day, to find some good to do—whether other people call it great or little. Whatever is done for the love of Jesus is a great thing greatly done in His eyes.

XLII

BUILDING

"Stone made ready before it was brought thither."
—1 KINGS vi. 7.

No builders like children! While men build huts and houses, you build castles, and while they must fix them on the ground, you can rear yours in the air! Men make noise and clatter enough when they are putting up the scaffolding, and are adding brick to brick and stone to stone, but you?—why, you simply shut your eyes, and the palace is finished, and every room is furnished with the sunbeams, too! Yet there has been no more noise about it than about the creeping of a shadow!

Since you are such good builders, then, I should almost apologise for venturing to speak on what you know so well. But I won't touch on what you are building, or mean to build; I only want to say a word on what is to be built *with* you—with you yourself—as if you were a beautiful stone, and not a beautiful boy or girl—as, of course, you all are!

Let me tell you something, then, about the great Temple at Jerusalem. It was built, as your castles in the air are built, without the least noise, though not quite so quickly as yours are. Everything was polished, and chiselled, and made ready before it was brought to the place where it was to be silently fitted; and so the Temple arose, quietly, beautifully as in a dream.

Something like this God is building now, and they are men and women, and boys and girls, He is building with. It isn't exactly a temple, or cathedral, such as those we have seen, yet it is something like in the way every person is put in the place that is best and most rightly fitted for him. But it is more like a great army, or a great place of business, where everybody finds his proper position according to what he really is and really can do, and not according to what he thinks he is, or thinks he can do. This is why we are all like stones which God is trying to shape and make ready now for the place He wants to put us in by-and-by.

The stones were cut, and chiselled, and polished in the quarry, far away from the Temple. It was very dark down there, and the stones must have found it very hard to understand why they were treated as they were. At first they were resting comfortably and undisturbed. Then the architect came along, looked thoughtfully round him, put a mark on a stone, said something to the workmen, and at once these set to work with their great hammers and crowbars, and never stopped till the block was lying on the ground, jagged, and rough, and shapeless.

After that other workmen chipped away at it till they had made it ever so much smaller and ever so much smoother; then other workmen rubbed and rubbed it with chips which had been broken from itself—always with chips broken from itself—till it was perfectly smooth and polished. Nor were the stones all of one shape, or after the same pattern. Some were square and some were curved, and some were big and some were little, some had ornaments and some were plain, and it must have been all very puzzling to the stones why this was so.

But by-and-by all was made clear. When they were carried away from the quarry, and every one was fitted into its proper place in the great Temple—then, when one stone curved a window, and another supported a pillar, and another stood on a pinnacle, like a spear-point flashing in the sunlight—then they understood all the meaning of the strange treatment which had been given them.

It is so with us now, and we shall never be rightly happy till we believe it. Every day God is trying to make us and shape us and fit us for something good, but what it is to be we shall never know till the time has come. There was Joseph: the chiselling was a bit hard on him when he was put in the pit and sold for a slave, and cast into prison, with false stories told about him—but how it all fitted him at last to become the great, patient, wise ruler of a kingdom! And there was David; scaring the birds from the wheat, and trudging about with the sheep—this didn't seem to be the way to make a king of him, but it was. You see, the king was *in* him, and this was the only way to bring him to show it. And there was Paul. He was very fond of reading and learning, and wanted to be a great scholar, so as to take a high place among men. He didn't know that God had set His mark on him, and was making him wish to be learned and wise because *He* meant to make use of his learning and wisdom by-and-by—as He did.

In the same way God has set His mark on some of you. You would like to be this and you would like to be that; you want to do this and you want to do that—and it is all right, if the thing itself is good. But one day God will put something in your way and ask you to do it for Him, and you will wonder, and ask yourself, "Can I do it?" Then, as you look back on all you have learnt, and all that you have done already, you will find that this is the very thing that you were being fitted for when least *you* meant it! Then do it, do it bravely, whatever it is, and God, Who was preparing you when you didn't know it, will help you still—as He helped Joseph, and David, and Paul.

Whatever happens to you day by day, whatever tasks are given you to learn, whatever duty is set you to do—whether the thing be big or little—think of God with it all, and take it all as a part of His training. This will help you to do well whatever you have to do, and, when the time comes, you will find it was all needed for the place God is keeping for you. So be true and faithful about little things; remember God in all—and leave the rest to Him. He will bring the stone from the quarry and fit it in its place of honour.

XLIII

NOT TOO PARTICULAR

"Where no oxen are, the crib is clean."—Prov. xiv. 4.

BE particular. Be *very* particular. If the train starts at 9.43, don't tell mother that it goes *about* a quarter to ten. She'll miss it, sure as anything! Be particular. *But don't be too particular!* Some people are; they must have everything just *so*, or be miserable. That's nothing, however, to the misery they can inflict on other folk! You understand this very well; there is nothing which gives you the fidgets so much as the ways of fidgety people. With them it is all, "Don't do this!" and, "Don't do that!" and, "Wipe your boots!" or, "Do sit still!" or, "Don't bang the door!" They are very particular, even on holidays. And don't they soak the spirit out of you! It is drizzle, drizzle, drizzle with them from morning to night, even when the sun is shining and there isn't a cloud in the sky.

There is a curious text in the Book of Proverbs about all this. You will find it in the fourth verse of the fourteenth chapter. It says: "Where no oxen are, the crib is clean." Only think of a cowherd who is crazy to have everything just *so!* The oxen do give him a deal of trouble; they are such careless, stupid things, poor creatures; they *will* drop their food out of the crib and litter it about, and they *will* scatter the straw in all directions; they *will* be untidy. Yet he wants to keep the byre like a new pin! But he will "best" them yet, the foolish creatures; they shall have no straw to lie on—that will keep the place neater. Moreover, he invents a new kind of crib, one that makes it difficult for the oxen to lift their food and scatter it about with their clumsy muzzles. Oh, it is very clever—very! He will cure them, too, of their habit of kicking over the pail; they shall have no water to drink except what he gives them himself at proper times. There's a byre for you!—there's a cowshed!—as clean as a granary and as sweet as nuts! The man is as pleased as Punch, and expects to get the first prize at the next Cattle Show.

But somehow or another the oxen don't thrive; they get thinner and thinner, weaker and weaker, and hang their heads lower and lower, as if they had something on their mind. And so they have; they are always wondering why they are so empty elsewhere! One after another they sicken and die, and when the last one has gone, the cowherd washes up the shed, and scrubs the cribs, and clears off all the litter, and feels quite happy, for now, at last, he can have everything just *so!* Yes, but the oxen are all gone; they have been improved out of the world by the one who who had charge of them being too particular.

Gain you wisdom by this. Be particular, but don't be too particular. If you have a rough stone wall to build, do not waste the day hunting for stones which will go all flush with one another, like bricks. Fit them in as best you can, with plenty of good mortar, but make allowance for one that sticks out a bit, and another that modestly shrinks in. And have a good deal of this mortar always ready when you come to deal with people. People are full of corners, cranks, edges, beauties, and flaws, and no two persons are exactly alike; you will only waste your time if you try to make them all like yourself. Of course, that would be best, if it could be done; but the trouble lies here—everybody wants to make *you* just like *himself*, for he thinks nobody could better that way of doing you good. So it can't be done. The best thing, then, is to use plenty of mortar. Can't you guess what the mortar is ?—kindness, charity, sympathy, love, appreciation. Mix these together and have them always ready, and though a great many things and a great many people to the very last won't be exactly what you would like them to be, yet you will keep a happy heart yourself, and will make the hearts of many others happy too. This is better—is it not ?—than having a clean crib because the oxen have all been starved, or having your own way about everything because you have killed off all your friends by being too particular.

There was a king once who retired from the business and gave himself up to the making of clocks. He made them very well, too, we are told—as a king should. But he caught the "particular" fever, and never quite got over it. His craze was this—to get all the clocks to tick at the same time—to keep step, as it were. But he couldn't manage it, king though he had been, and it nearly "worritted" him into his grave. Now, people are like these clocks; they will do their duty (the best of them, any way) and come up to time, but you must let every one have his own tick.

How many mothers there are who used to nag, and scold, and fret continually because they couldn't get this little fellow or that little girlie to be particular! But when the little one was taken from them, when the crib was empty, what would they not have given to see the toys littered about again, the crumbs on the carpet, and the marks of the little muddy feet on the lobby! Where no children are the house is tidy, but we would rather have the children, with their fun and their frolic, though it *does* try the patience to put things to rights after they've gone to bed, the monkeys!

So be particular, but don't be too particular. Never forget that where there is life there will always be some litter, and wherever there are people there will always be something which could be improved to the very last. So be big-hearted, be kindly, be charitable, and make allowances for other people; as for yourself, and for all you have to do, fix this in your mind:—

>   That man is blest
>   Who does his best,
>   And leaves the rest,
>   *And doesn't worry.*

XLIV

THE TEMPTER

> "Again there was a day when the sons of God came to present themselves before the Lord, and Satan came also among them, to present himself before the Lord. And the Lord said unto Satan, From whence comest thou? And Satan answered the Lord, and said, From going to and fro in the earth, and from walking up and down in it."—JOB. ii. 1, 2.

HERE is a strange picture, somewhat odd and startling, but one which you have all seen again and again, though maybe you don't recognise it at the first glance.

Who are "the sons of God"? You are one—a son or a daughter of God, if you are loving the Lord Jesus and have given your heart to Him.

But what about "presenting themselves before the Lord"? Have *you* never done that? You have—many and many a time. For, whenever you come to worship—to pray to the Lord and praise Him—that is presenting yourself before Him, just as the great ones of the land present themselves before the Queen. The Lord is always present whenever two or three gather together in His name. Whenever we meet for worship we meet with the Lord, if we have come with the right heart, for the right purpose. So, you see, this is nothing new—God's children presenting themselves before Him.

They never do this — never worship and praise God—but there is somebody with them they would be better without. It is Satan. Yes, children, the devil goes to church, but it is not to worship, not to pray; it is to keep you from worshipping and praying if he can. I have never seen him, but I have known him to be very near. When my eyes have been shut and I have been trying to tell God in prayer what the poor, sad, sinful souls of men and women and children are needing, I have sometimes hardly been able to do it, because Satan has been near me, jingling keys in his pocket, rattling his watch-chain, turning over the leaves of his hymn-book, or shuffling with his feet. *He* wasn't praying; he took care to let me know that; and he made me know only too well that I wasn't praying either, as I would have liked to pray. And sometimes, when I have been preaching, I have seen him at work, busy, busy, very busy. There is a lad at my left; he has sat gaping and gazing all over the church, to see who was there whom he knew; and there is a lady on my right who has not been able to listen to a word of the sermon through thinking of the new dress somebody before her has got. There are two foolish boys at the back who whisper and grin through all the service; and there is a man at the front who keeps buying and selling many things in his mind, even when he looks most devout. And there is a man in the pulpit who thinks sometimes that this is clever or that is neat, when he should rather be asking, Is it true? is it kind? is it right? is it what God would wish him to say, or is it only what will please the people? Ah, yes, children! we never meet to worship but Satan presents himself too. Sometimes he comes late, and knocks the books from the pew-board as he gets to his seat. I have even known him disturb a person in prayer rather than reverently wait a minute. But there is no reverence in him. When the Lord asks, "Whence comest thou?" his answer is simple impudence — "From going to and fro in the earth, and from walking up and down in it." That wasn't an answer; that didn't tell where he had been; it never mentioned a place or gave an address; it was simply impertinence. He might just as well have said that he came from "the Back of Beyond."

There is no place in all the world where we can get rid of Satan. He goes to church, he stands beside us when we kneel and pray, and tries to draw our thoughts away from the Lord; there is never a time and never a spot but he is near us. Yet we can't see him, and we often forget that he is near. How can we keep him, then, from doing us harm? There is only one way: by letting Jesus have the keeping of our hearts. Nobody else can protect us. Satan wanted to get Peter, and nearly got him, too; but Jesus prayed for the tempted man, and that saved him. Give your heart to Jesus, then; love Him, trust Him, and live for the things he loves, and Satan will never harm you; you will be kept by the power of Jesus for salvation. May He deliver us all from the Evil One!

XLV

NEAT KNOTS

"Sins that are past."—Rom. iii. 25.

I WAS taken over a great weaving factory once, where there were hundreds of steam-looms, which seemed to know all they were about, and went on doing their work with hardly any attention given them. One person would have three or four of these machines under his care, so easy were they to manage. But while I was looking and admiring, one of the machines stopped suddenly, and the man who had charge of it gave a quick glance at the thousands of threads, and took one of them up. It had broken—and it was its breaking that had made all stop, for these machines are made so finely that if a single thread snaps it will stop everything, and so give warning to the workman of the mishap. He drew out the bobbin a little farther, tied the thread in a particular way and place, and the machine was set going as before.

Then I learnt something. If the machine had been allowed to go on with that thread broken, the whole web—the piece that was being woven—would have been spoiled; for not only would the blank bit have been noticed, but it would have weakened all the rest, and would have grown wider and wider the more the piece was used.

It is the same with the "sins that are past." They may be past—be behind us in time—may have been done weeks or months or years ago—but if they have not been mended and put right, they have been all that time doing harm to us. Our hearts have been made harder, the love and the trust of Jesus has gone away more and more from us, we don't see what is good as we once saw it, and we don't care to be good as we once did.

We need Jesus to put right what has gone wrong. He can do it. When we are really sorry for our sins, and pray to Him, and want to have wrong things put right, He can do it; He can pardon what we have done, but He can do something more—He can make it turn out for good.

A good workman, with one of the machines of which I have been speaking, is not satisfied with tying again the thread that has become broken. He studies how to tie it so that it shall not only hold firm, but that it shall also be for beauty, rather than for blemish. If there is any raised ornament in the pattern, he ties the knot so that it shall fit in there; then it not only is no longer seen as a bit that is broken, but it even helps that part of the pattern.

Jesus is wonderfully skilful with the "sins that are

past." He can not only put right what has gone wrong, but He can make it turn out for good. There was a man I knew who, in a fit of bad temper, cut his hand very deep. He was ashamed of his temper, went and prayed to Jesus, and never since has he been so foolish; he says that as soon as he sees the scar on his hand he remembers his prayer, and that keeps him from being so angry again. He is now one of the most patient men I know; Jesus not only tied up the broken thread, as it were, but He tied it so as to make it be for beauty, rather than for ugliness.

That is how He would use all our sins that are past. We can't reach back to them, but He can; and He can not only put them right, but He can also make them turn to our good.

Then bring them all to Him. Stop—as the machine stops—when you have done anything that is wrong, and at once pray to Jesus to have it put right. Don't let it go on; that is only to make trouble for yourself and others in the future, for every sin that is not put right frays away, and frays away, and spoils us in the end. Go to Jesus at once when you have done anything wrong; He, and He only, can make it really past —clean gone for ever in its power to harm ourselves or other people.

XLVI

THE SCENT OF LIFE

"In the Spirit."—REV. i. 10.

PERHAPS you won't just catch at the first what this means—"In the Spirit." But you know what it is to be in different kinds of *moods*. Sometimes you are in a good mood, sometimes in a bad one: sometimes you are in a bright mood, sometimes in a dumpish one. At one time you feel strong and well and full of energy, and then you say, "I am in a mood to work to-day;" but at another time you feel weak and dull and stupid, and you say, "I am not in a working mood." At times you will sing like a lark, and listen so eagerly while others are singing; but there are times again when you won't sing yourself, and when it only makes you sad to hear others singing; you are in no mood for songfulness just then.

Now, what is a mood? *It is the scent of the Spirit.* How can you tell one flower from another in the dark? Isn't it by the scent? You sniff and sniff, and say, "This is a violet, that is mignonette, that is lavender, and that is — pugh! wild onion — how nasty!" You don't need to see the flowers, you don't need to touch them; the scent is quite sufficient to tell you what kind they are.

It is the same with moods: they always tell what kind of a spirit is in you—a good spirit or a bad one, a sad spirit or a glad one, a kind or an unkind one, for moods are the scent of the spirit.

One day Jesus stood watching some children playing in the market-place. They were a merry little company, and got on very well for a while, till some of them began to push the others roughly, or say unkind things, and that made these become cross and sulky; but the ones who pushed were quite bright. The people who push are always bright, and quite ready to push again; but the people who are pushed are apt to feel things a little differently, and so the little merry company came to be divided into two— those who were in a bright mood and those who were in a sulky one. And the bright ones said, "Come, let us have a dance," and they whistled and piped, and made believe they were a royal band. But the others would not dance; never a shuffle would they make with their feet. They were in a sulky mood— and people cannot dance when they are sulky, for if they did they would lose their sulkiness! Then the others said, "Well, if you won't play at dancing, let us play at mourning—let us have funerals." But the others would not play at that either. That showed as clear as noonday what kind of a spirit was in them

—it was a sore, sad, vexed, and injured spirit. And as Jesus looked upon them He said there were people like them; their spirit was all wrong, for the mood they were in showed the spirit that was in them.

It always does. If we are in a bad mood, it is because we have a bad spirit in us; if we are in a good mood, it is because we have a good spirit. So you see, if we are ever to have right moods, right fancies, or right thoughts, we must begin by being "in the spirit" of all that is right and good.

Now, I think, you will be better able to understand what it is to be "in the spirit" of anything. It means to be in thorough sympathy with it. Suppose you are vexed and cross and angry, and then sit down to write a nice, kind letter to a little friend who is far away, and lonely and down-hearted, could you do it? No, you could not — not then. If you wrote while that angry spirit was in you your letter would not be a comforting one; it would be cold and harsh and hard. Or again, when you are loving and kind and good, could you sit down and write an angry and spiteful letter? No, you couldn't: the sharp words wouldn't come; there would still be honey rather than vinegar in the ink. And it is the same about everything; everything we do, and everything we think and say, depends on whether we are "in the spirit" of it or not.

John was "in the Spirit of the Lord on the Lord's day," and oh! what a blessed, blessed day that was for him! He saw right away into heaven, and he heard sweet voices speaking to him from the skies. But if he hadn't been in the spirit of the day he would not have seen or heard anything of all that. When you come to church, flushed, and hot, and late—oh! it is hard, hard, to get a good thought planted in your heart, just because you are not in the spirit of the Lord's Day. But when you come from prayer, and come quietly and prayerfully, thinking of Jesus, then good thought upon good thought steals into the heart, and you are stronger and brighter and braver all the week. Children, children, there is no blessing for anybody in all the world till he comes himself to be "in the spirit" of the blessing.

What, then, are we to do when we are not in the right spirit? Just this: *change the gearing.* There are bicycles that have two ways of going—a hard way and an easy one. The hard way is the swift way, and that does finely on a level road, but it is very difficult to go up a stiff hill with it. Then they change the gearing, as they call it; they press a little handle, and that takes the stiffness out of the wheels, so that they can go up the hill quite easily. You must learn to change the gearing. You may be in a very good and pleasant spirit so long as there is nothing to vex you or try your temper, or make you sad, but when any of these things come in your way, then how hard you find it to keep in a good spirit! That is the time to change the gearing, the time to pray, and pray, and pray—oh, how earnestly!—for the Lord to help you, for the Lord to remember you and keep you, and put His—His very own—Spirit in you. Do that, and though the Hill Difficulty may be hard to climb, you will climb it, and be in the right spirit all the way. So, whenever the mood you are in shows that you are in a naughty spirit, lift your heart up to Jesus. Directly you speak to Him or come close to Him the naughty spirit will depart from you. Love Him, and love Him again, and love Him more still, for we always come quickest into the spirit of any one when we love.

XLVII

OPEN SECRETS

"Dark sayings."—Ps. lxxviii. 2.

This is a curious expression. Did you ever see "a saying"? I never did. I have heard a good many sayings in my time, but I never saw one. Perhaps it was there all the time and I could not see it because I was searching for it like the nigger boy looking for a black cat in a dark cellar without a light! But, after all, I don't think that could be the reason. You cannot see a "say" as you can see a saw; we must seek for the meaning in another direction.

There is a statue of Shakespeare set up in Leicester Square, and this quotation is carved upon it: "There is no darkness but ignorance." That is true. God is perfectly wise, and therefore there is nothing hidden from Him; He is perfectly wise, and so understands all things. A "dark saying," then, just means something we cannot make out. But the fault may not be in the saying—the fault may be in us; we haven't brought the light with us.

There is a name we have for these dark sayings; we call them *riddles*. How dark a riddle is at first! You can't see through it. But when you do discover it at last, what do you say? Isn't it this?—"Ah! I *see* it now!" And then how foolish you feel—foolish to think you had been so long in seeing what, after all, was so plain! The riddle was a riddle till you brought the key; but the key had been in your own head all the time if you could only have got at it quicker.

But there is another name we sometimes give to these dark sayings. We call them *secrets*. Do you know the difference between a riddle and a secret? It is the difference between finding and exploring. When you discover a riddle you discover it all at once—there is a flash, as it were, an idea, and you have got it. But it is different with a secret. You have to dig for that as men dig for gold and silver, and when you have got it, it doesn't look like gold or silver, but like copper or iron; you have to learn how to melt it and get it out. Or you have to master it as men master the Greek and the Hebrew—by learning a little bit, and a little bit more, every day; understanding a little bit, and a little bit more, every day. The work has to go on inside yourself before you can come to read quite plainly what had been such a strange, mysterious secret to you before. And then, most likely, after years and years of hard study you laugh quietly to yourself, and say, "Where is the secret? There is none! It is all plain and open to me; I wonder how I ever could have thought there was any mystery about it." Yes, it was your ignorance that made the darkness; the darkness was in you and not in the sayings.

It is the same with everything. God has to teach us. It is dark or quite plain just as we bring or do not bring the right light to it. *He* has not hidden anything from us; things are hidden from us just as the Hebrew or Greek may be hidden from us. We may see the letters but yet not understand their meaning, because we haven't tried to train ourselves for it.

Do you remember how, when David was in danger, his friend Jonathan gave him a warning? Jonathan was watched, and therefore could not go and speak to David, but he had agreed about a signal to give him. So Jonathan went out into the field and began to shoot arrows. If you had seen him then you would simply have thought he was amusing himself. But David from his hiding-place was watching, and by the way the arrows went he learnt that Saul was seeking for his life. He was in the secret, and Jonathan was in the secret, but to everybody else it was only an idle game. Yet there was such a deep meaning in it all.

And that is how it is with all that is around us.

God has a meaning in everything. He is trying to signal to us through everything; but we can get at His meaning only as we have been let into His secret. It is a secret, and yet it is not a secret; it is quite plain, and yet there is only one who can understand it. Who is that? It is the boy or the girl, the man or the woman, who fears God. "The secret of the Lord is with them that fear Him." To fear Him doesn't mean to be afraid of Him. It is quite the other way; it means to love Him, to trust Him, to keep on thinking about Him, to lift the heart to Him in everything—to remember God in all our ways. As we do that we are learning *God* as we would learn a language. The Bible, the world, our own hearts, Jesus, everything becomes clearer and simpler, and easier to understand; the darkness goes as we bring more light, but the light must come from our own hearts. It is the fear of the Lord that is the beginning of wisdom—a wisdom that is more than knowledge and better than knowledge—the wisdom that cometh down from above.

Children, keep your hearts always towards God. Be reverent in everything about Him; be humble, willing to learn; above all, be trustful. The teacher cannot teach anything unless the child believes what he says, and God cannot teach us or "enlighten" us unless we do the same.

How do you see the sun? It is because the sun is shining; the sun gives the light by which you see the light. And just so it is only God who can show us God. Then begin with Him, continue with Him, end with Him about everything, and His darkest sayings will become very, very bright, and their brightness will make up the eternal daytime of your soul.

XLVIII

HOW TO BEGIN THE DAY

"It is a good thing to give thanks unto the Lord, and to sing praises unto Thy name, O most High: to show forth Thy loving-kindness in the morning, and Thy faithfulness every night."—Ps. xcii. 1, 2.

YES, it is a good thing; you may not be able to know at the time why, yet it is a good thing—good for you, and good for everybody round you—to begin and end the day with God.

It is good in the morning—for it gives us the right keynote for the day.

You are singers—very nice singers, too, some of you—and you know something about music. Do you know what *flattening* means? It is like this: sometimes, when people are singing, they forget what the right sound should be, and all their notes get lower and lower, for the one has to push the other down so as to make it keep its proper distance; and the worst of it is, the singer has no idea of how far he has gone wrong, till he hears the keynote struck: then he knows!

That is just the way with people who try to get on without God; without thinking of Him in the morning.

without praying to Him, or reading a bit of His Word. The music of their life keeps going down and down—it *flattens;* and the worst of it is, they don't know it. Others observe it; people round them can tell it, but they can't themselves, for they don't listen for the keynote. Be you wiser; make sure of this—that it is a good thing to begin with God in the morning. That will help you to keep your heart high and right all through the day.

And it is a good thing to end the day with God. You are going to forget Him, and forget everybody for a little, while you sleep. But He is not going to forget you; it would be a bad, bad thing for you if He did. He is going to watch over you in the night, just as He did through the day. Think of that! God standing like a faithful sentinel to protect you when you cannot protect yourself! Will you go to sleep without thanking Him? without thinking of Him? without one loving word for Him? That's *not* good, not kind; and nobody can grow up right, or strong, or wise, or loving who does that.

So end the day as you begin it, by having a little time alone with God, and though you may not be able now to know why, by-and-by, when you grow up, when you know things better and see them clearer, you too will say—and say it, oh! with such a glad and grateful heart—"It was *good* for me to begin and end all my days with God!"

XLIX

DON'T GROW OLD

NEVER grow old. It's a bad habit, and shouldn't be yielded to. But it's worse to grow sour or crabbed or conceited. Let me tell you something about all this.

I once lay down one beautiful summer day on the mossy carpet of a little copse-wood, and by-and-by—whether I was asleep or whether I was awake doesn't matter—I heard two trees beside me begin to talk. The one was a tall and stately oak, which had borne the buffets of the storms for more than a hundred years, and the other was a little oak sapling, which had seen only about half-a-dozen summers. Of course it must have seen as many winters too, but it made no account of these; the summers were all that it remembered or cared about, and just now its bright yellow leaves were toying and frolicking with the sunshine—which left some of the gold from its own beams on every leaf it kissed. Very soon, however, the sunshine disappeared, and when the sapling looked up and saw the reason it suddenly became very quiet and still, and I think it was also a little timid, for the old oak was bending a great branch over it in a most reproving way, and was looking very severe.

"When are you going to learn a little sense?" asked the old oak, in a gruff and very timbery voice. "Here you are doing nothing but playing with the sunbeams and hooraying with your leaves after every breeze: isn't it time you were putting away all that foolishness and learning something of what the life of an oak should be? Why can't you be sedate, as I am? Your leaves are given you for something else than flicking the sunshine; *I* am always feeling with mine for the coming storm, so that I may give warning to the flowers to close their petals, and to the birds to seek for shelter, but *you* never think of that; *you* can't tell a storm yet when it is only three minutes away from you. Besides, you are putting too much sunshine on your leaves; they look too gaudy; it is time you were learning to lay up some sunshine inside your bark to keep you warm in the winter, instead of spending it all in vain show. You are too dressy—far too dressy; why can't you be sober and sombre like me? Believe me, my young friend, life is a very serious thing for a thoughtful tree;" and the old oak raised its branch again in a dignified fashion, as much as to say, "Open rebuke is better than secret flattery."

How frightened the little sapling was! It actually stood rooted to the ground with fear! But it wasn't for long; the sunbeams came back when the shadow of the big branch was removed, and almost before it knew what it was doing it was laughing and toying and frisking with them just as before, which only made the old oak stiffen its dignity more than ever.

Presently some laughing, shouting, ruddy-faced children came tumbling into the wood, and with a cry of delight made for the sapling. "Look! look! —leaves of gold! Let's take some home to Willie," said the eldest; "he always says he forgets he's sick when he has got flowers and leaves and things to make up;" and in a perfect ecstasy they plucked the spoils from the sapling, and proud, glad, and happy was the little tree that it had something to give to cheer the lonely hours of a sick and weary child. And the old oak suddenly flurried its branches as if it had just found out a big mistake it had made, but didn't like to say so.

You see—and this is the point of the story—the old oak was a sapling once itself; indeed it was, though you wouldn't think so to see it now; and then it had ever so much fun and frolic inside its ribs, and was a good bit dressy, too—dressy with sunshine. But it had forgotten all that; it had got into the bad habit of growing old. Take a warning by it. Never grow old; you have no occasion to. It isn't the number of years we live that makes us old. The youngest people I've ever known were over seventy! Yes; yet they were still young, very young, fond of children, fond of kittens and little puppies (four-footed ones, of course), and young plants, and everything else that was just starting in the business of living. These dear folks never grew old; they had fortunately lost the recipe, and so they couldn't find out how to become crabbed or sour or stuck-up. Learn to be like them, and begin now. Because you are twelve, and can read and write, don't turn up your dear little nose at the queer sprawling and spelling of the seven-year-older. You once made as many blots yourself, and were just as much puzzled about Con-stan-ti-no-ple. And when you grow older—out of knickers or short frocks, and into tall hats or wonderful bonnets—don't get out of sympathy, out of love or interest for the little ones; don't pretend you weren't one of them once yourself, for nobody will believe you.

It was only a little clod the gardener held in his hand, yet he wondered at it. "Why do you smell so sweet?" he asked; and the answer which the clod made was as beautiful as it was humble—"Because once a rose grew in me." Do you see the meaning? The clod, though it was only a clod, knew how to carry about with it always the sweetness of days that were gone, and so it was always sweet itself. Try to do the same. Forget what is bad, remember what is good, and you'll never grow old though you live to the age of Methuselah.

L

"*WHEN HE COMETH.*"

"They shall be Mine, saith the Lord of hosts, in that day when I make up My jewels."—MAL. iii. 17.

"WHEN He cometh, when He cometh!"—who doesn't know that hymn? Who doesn't love it, and love it best of all when tiny wee children lisp it or sing it? There is a lilt about it and a tenderness, like the songs the birds sing when the sun is going down—songs that say, "Though the darkness may come up for a time, the light will return in the morning."

There is such a longing and loving in it all! Away beyond the tossing waves, in a far-off land, there is a brave young fellow, with sunburnt face and brawny arms, working with a will from sunrise to sunset. It was expedient for those at home here that he should go away, for times were bad with them, work was scarce, and they could hardly get bread. And he went away, with tears in his eyes and a big lump in his throat, but determined to do well by those he had left behind. And he did, and sent them help, and was coming back one day with enough for them all. It was very hard with them at home sometimes. They could just manage to get on when the winter was cold and the ground was hard, and work was scarce, and sickness was about. But they were cheerful, cheerful, wondrously cheerful, for there was one song that was never for long away from their hearts. It was this: "When he cometh, when he cometh——!" You see, they were living in hope. They believed in the brave young heart that had gone away for them, and they were always looking for the ship with the silver sails that would bring him back again, and then—no more hunger, no more cold, no more faintness or pinch or want. What was it that kept up their hearts? It was Hope!

And that is the music of a song like this and the words that make it. It is Hope, bright Hope, that trembles and sparkles through it all. "They shall be Mine, saith the Lord of hosts," when He cometh. "Mine, My own, My very own—My jewels!"

Learn, children, to sing that song, and sing it with meaning—sing it with Hope. If there is anything that can make the heart glad and the life strong and beautiful, it is having something good and bright and gladsome to look forward to. And what can be better than this: when all is over and done here, when our day's work is finished, and we have to say good-bye to everybody, because we are going away—away—out of this world altogether—that then—*then*—this should be our sure comfort—the Lord will keep us, the Lord will take care of us, for we are *His?* "They shall be Mine!" Then, if we belong to the Lord, who can hurt us? What can harm us? Nothing! No one! The Lord is Almighty: none can snatch away from Him what is His own.

Are you His, my boy? Are you His, my girl? There is only one way of being His, and that is by giving one's self altogether to Jesus. Have you done that? Have you asked Him to take you and make you His very own? If you have, then you are one of God's jewels.

Keep this in mind, and it will explain a lot. Nothing gets more cuts and rubs than a jewel does. There is not much beauty about a diamond at first. If you didn't know better, you would most likely toss it away. But how careful men are about it when they know it to be a diamond! And the first thing they do is to cut it! Yes, cut it—cutting away all the black stuff that was round it, and that was keeping back the light that was in it. And it is all very puzzling to the diamond; if this is kindness, it thinks, the kindness is strange. And so it is at first; but by-and-by, when the jewel has been cut, and rubbed, and polished, how brilliant it becomes! how beautiful! It is set in the finest gold and becomes a present for a king.

Yet you are worth more than all the diamonds in the world. And the Lord wants to make you and shape you, till you become like a jewel flashing on His crown. So He must do with you as men do with the diamond—give you many a rub, and many a stroke, and many a deep cutting besides. And the tears will come, and you will sometimes wonder very much what it all means. That is the time to sing the song, "When He cometh, when He cometh——!" For then all will be explained, then the brightness will shine out, then you will find there was love in it all; it was because you were His own, His very own, He was determined to make the best of you that could be made.

So sing the song, and sing it in your heart, and sing it all your days, and always sing it with a loving, trustful look up to the heavens—

> "When He cometh, when He cometh,
> To make up His jewels,—
>
> Like the stars of the morning,
> His bright crown adorning,
> They shall shine in their beauty,
> Bright gems for His crown."

LI

AN IMPROBABLE STORY

PERHAPS you won't like it any the worse for being improbable. Probable stories are as thick as blackberries in September, but improbable stories are as rare as swallows in winter. There is, besides, a good deal of improbability about the time when it occurred. It has something to do with Christmas—if you can make out what that "something" is—yet it was in the high summer-time that the thing happened. But when is Christmas done? Not before next Christmas. When is it begun? Last Christmas, and the Christmas before that, and the one before that again. "Christmas comes but once a year," but it comes—or should come—to let its spirit linger with us through all the year. This is the story: if it reads like a riddle, the sharper minds will like it the better for having to think twice to make it out.

Frankie was a choir-boy, and as good as they make them. It was a very hot afternoon when he was left to keep house because his mother and sister were paying some visits. He had amused himself with one thing and another, and at last had tried a stave or two of a curious Christmas carol he had found in an old book kicked out of its place under the leg of a side-table, where it was put to keep things steady. But some of the words were odd—half-Frenchy. Some of the notes were difficult, and with an impatient jerk he tossed the book down and—upset his whole case of silkworms! What a panic there was amongst the creatures! There they were, wriggling and writhing in all manner of frantic contortions, and do what he would, he could not stop their agitation. With a feather he carefully replaced them all, speaking soothing words the while, but his voice only seemed to frighten them the more; perhaps they thought it was thunder—thunder following a kind of earthquake! Frank was sorry; he was fond of his worms; he had reared them year after year, and had given every one its own name—or rather the name of some deacon in the chapel or master in the school—and it was very remarkable how well the names and the natures seemed to fit one another, even when fixed on these creepy, crawly things. So much for what's in a name! It was no use calling them by name now, however; the things were clearly frightened, and Frankie felt how helpless he was to assure them of his goodwill. If he could only get them to understand!

He had thrown himself down on the couch to think the thing over, which means that he soon fell asleep. And then the rosy cloud hovered before him, and though he could not see who was in it, he could hear the voice.

And when the voice asked, he answered and said he would like above everything to be able to comfort the silkworms. Then a hand came forth from the rosy cloud and touched his brow, and the spot gleamed like a fair, soft star. When the star shone, said the voice, he would be able to return again as he went.

Before Frank had time to guess what was meant he found himself in the case with the silkworms. But, strangest of all, he was now one himself! A tiny spark of light glowed from his head; nothing like it was in any other. As he glided along he came upon some worms that were eagerly gathering into little heaps every scrap of mulberry-leaf they could find; they were the anxious ones, always living in dread of perishing for want of food. He assured them there was no need for their anxiety; he was their master, and would see that they had all that they needed day by day. But they hardly gave him a glance, let alone listened, they were so anxiously searching about. But some again were rude and wild, and stole what the others had gathered, and fought against them and bit them. And when Frank said "Shame!" and bid them be gentle, they turned on him and attacked him fiercely. They never saw the light that was glowing from him; they were so blinded with passion. He had barely escaped when he came upon some who were lying very still and looking very sad. They were about to die, they explained; in a little while they would weave their silken shrouds round about them, and then they would be no more. Frankie tried to comfort them. They would not die, he said; they would only sleep and swoon away—swoon away into a beautiful butterfly, with wings of amber and gold, to flit through the sunny air from flower to flower, over scented fields. These listened to him; they saw the light, and they asked him to tell them more, and his words were sweeter than music to them against the time when they would have to shape their shrouds. But the wild and wicked ones returned and mocked him, and then they grew angrier and angrier still, and closed round him, and together they attacked him fiercely.

When he awoke he arose from the couch and leaned very long and very thoughtfully over his case of silk-worms. There was many a curious thought going on in his mind, which, being only a boy, he could not very well express. But at last he took up very reverently the book he had so impatiently tossed away, and he found the carol, and found he could sing it, too, for it wasn't so difficult now as it had been before.

And that is the improbable story. Whatever can it mean?

LII

DICKY BOY

"The star, which they saw in the east, went before them, till it came and stood over where the young child was."—MATT. ii. 9.

THIS was long, long ago, and they were great men, wise men, rich men, who came out of the land where Abraham was born, and came into the land where Abraham lived, and came by the light of the Star-beam to Mary and Joseph—and JESUS.

I can't tell you much more about these men, for there isn't very much more told us; but I can tell you about Dicky Boy, and it is all about him I am going to write.

He lived down Bermondsey way, and lived in a stable. You would think from this that he was a horse or an ass, but he wasn't the one or the other. Dicky Boy was a boy, and he was eight years old at that business; but he lived in a stable all the same, his mother and he together, up in a hayloft; but there was a partition made with old boards between where the hay was kept and their dining-room, and drawing-room, and kitchen, and bedroom, for they were all one. There were three stalls in the stable below, where three ponies were kept, but the three ponies were seldom for long at home together; they were like three-volume novels at a seaside place—when the one was in the others were out, and when the others were in the one was out—you seldom got the set complete. What their business was doesn't matter; they came and went at all hours, and it was needful that somebody should be about to open the door when the dogcarts came back, and so Dicky Boy's mother had that apartment given to her upstairs next door to the hay, and she had it rent free for minding the door.

It was a queer little bunk of a place. A tall man could stand straight up in the middle, but only a very little child could stand up at the wall where the window was; for the roof sloped down three different ways, and there was just wall enough for a little window on one side. Away in the darkest corner there was a bed on the floor, and in the opposite corner there was a kind of table with dishes and things, and in the middle was the fireplace over against the partition. That partition was beautifully papered with newspapers, and a picture of an execution, and one long coloured strip of the Lord Mayor's Show. That picture used to be Dicky's delight; if the procession had ever got mixed, Dicky could have put it all together again, for he knew exactly where the band should be, and the trumpeters, and which coach came first and which was last—he had got it all by heart.

But one day there was an event in the hayloft which

gave a new joy to Dicky. Mother had gone round to the chandler's for a loaf, and when she came back she had a picture with her. It *was* a picture, and no mistake; and when it was pinned up on the partition it made the place quite gorgeous. What a sight! and what colouring! A great yellow desert, stretching away to a golden Star that was making long shadows to half-a-dozen pyramids in the distance, while a number of men, with turbans and cloaks and camels, were gazing on the Star and travelling towards it. Oh, it was a beautiful picture! And underneath it was the text, "The Star went before them," and then in fine big letters came the words, "Muggins' Mustard is THE BEST." Dicky could not read, but he soon knew the words by heart, for mother told him; and the yellow desert, they both agreed, had something to do with Muggins' mustard. But that didn't signify. There was "the Star that went before them," and there were the men and their camels following it.

Dicky could not get that Star out of his head, and many a talk mother and he had over it when she sat at the little table sewing; for she sewed a great deal, mother did, both by the window-light and by candle-light—she was always sewing. And Dicky was never tired of asking questions and hearing about that Star, and somehow or other all that they said always came round to the same thing; they both agreed that "there's a deal of good to be got by following the Star." That was a remark that got into Dicky's head too—got in almost as far as the Star itself—and whatever else he was sure of, or whatever else he didn't know, he was sure of this, that "there's a deal of good to be got by following the Star."

Mother's cough had been very troublesome, and when the snow began to fall, and the frost had made the roads slippery for the ponies, her cough grew worse and worse, till sometimes she had scarcely any breath left in her poor thin body. But her eyes were always so bright—as bright, Dicky thought, as the Star—and sometimes there was such a red, red spot on her cheek. And she had to take to her bed oftener, and Dicky had oftener to get up in the night and open the door for the ponies. One night he had slipped down in the dark to do this, and when he crept upstairs again, he found the candle lighted and mother out of bed. "Come here, Dicky Boy," she said; "I want you to kneel down with me before the Star." And the two together, their arms round one another, knelt down there, while mother sobbed and prayed. Then she kissed him on the brow—oh, such a long, kind kiss! "Dicky dear," she said, "I am going away—away to follow the Star; and you will promise me one thing, won't you?—that you will follow the Star too. Oh, there is such a deal of good to be got by following the Star!" Dicky didn't answer her; he didn't know what to say; and they lay down together again to sleep. She slept so long, mother did, that though Dicky had gone up and down twice to open the door, she hadn't awoke. He had got a cup of tea ready for her at the little fire, and had waited, waited; and at last he called her, so quietly and gently; but she still slept on. Then he took her hand, and it was so cold; and he kissed her, but her lips were cold too; and he got frightened, and began to cry, and went downstairs to the man who was grooming the pony, and asked him if he would come upstairs and waken mother. And the man went up, and when he came down he had a strange look on his face.

"You come with me," he said kindly, taking Dicky's hand in his own big rough one, and leading him out.

"Is mother awake?" Dicky asked.

"Ay, ay," said the man in a thick, kind voice, "she's awake enough; she's better now."

And that was the last Dicky saw of his mother. Bridget O'Halloran, the Irishwoman down the lane, with the six children and the loud, scolding voice took Dicky into her house, and he slept with the "childer," and got scolded with them too; but somehow Bridget's eyes would fill with tears as she scolded him (it was all through the weather, she said), and it was because he was such a weak bit of a boy that she always let him have the biggest share.

Little by little Dicky found out that his mother was dead. But nobody could tell him where she was buried. The O'Halloran children had seen a black coach go from a neighbour's house, and it went *that* way; that was all they knew. And *that* way Dicky went too. He didn't know why his little heart was like a stone; he never saw the crowds, nor heard the rumble and the noise; he just knew one thing—mother had gone *that* way, and mother had gone to follow the Star, and mother wanted him to follow it too, and he did want to see mother again. It's such a poor little world, this of ours, when mother's away!

But what with the turnings and the twistings, he got lost at last. He would need to ask his way. So he looked at people's faces, watching for a kind one, and found one, a big sailor, rigged out in a new suit that didn't fit him, and with such a big pipe in his mouth.

"If you please, sir," said Dicky, "can you tell me the way to the East?"

"Well, I never!" said the big fellow, lifting his eyebrows. "What an insult! A little chit like you to suppose I never learnt to box the compass, and me been round the world a dozen times! Could I tell you the way to the East? Why, that's good!" And he took such a hearty guffaw as if the thing were the best joke he had heard.

"Beg your pardon, sir," said Dicky timidly, "but I didn't mean no harm."

"And no more you've done it," said the sailor. "But what do you want to know the way to the East for?"

"'Cause the Star's there," said Dicky, "and mother's gone after the Star."

"Has she? Well, she must be a bright 'un! What kind of star has she gone after?"

"It's the Star that leads to Jesus—'The Star which went before them,'" Dicky eagerly said.

"Look here, my lad," said the sailor, turning grave, "you stow all that, will you? Fun's fun, but you shan't speak of Jesus that way. Where's your mother?"

"I don't know," said Dicky sadly; "but she's dead, and gone after the Star, and I'm going to follow it too."

"I can't make you out, youngster," said the sailor gently, "but you look a good boy, and your mother's dead. All right; here's something for you, and that's the East;" and he put some coppers into Dicky's hand, and jerked with his thumb over his shoulder and walked away, but only to stop and look back, and look back again, and then stand looking very thoughtfully after Dicky till the boy disappeared. Then, taking the pipe from his mouth, and knocking the ashes out on his heel, the sailor pulled himself straight, buttoned his coat, and went off at a quick step, as if to do something he had made up his mind for.

But Dicky went on—on and on—street after street, road over road, this side and that side, like a little doggie that had lost his master, till he came to the river down Deptford way. It was getting so dark now, and the river looked so cold, and its banks were so ugly, that he was glad to find a snug spot near the wharf where some bales were waiting to be shipped, and he crept among them for warmth and shelter. Presently a young man came near, shivering with cold, and looking wretched in the fading light. He had a look about him of a clerk who had been gambling with his master's money; but Dicky didn't know what a clerk was, or gambling either. The man walked several times down to the edge of the water, and then came slowly, hesitatingly back; but at last he took a paper and pencil from his pocket, and going up to one of the bales where Dicky was, began to write. Just then Dicky moved, and the man got such a fright!

"I beg your pardon, sir," said Dicky; "I did't mean to frighten you."

"What are you doing there?" the man asked sharply.

"I was just resting a bit," said the boy, "before going on again."

"Going on where?"

"To the East."

"To the East? What East?"

"I don't know, sir," said Dicky. "It's the East where the Star is."

"What Star?"

"The one as leads to Jesus. 'The Star went before them,'" he said simply, as if that explained everything; "and mother's dead, and gone after the Star to Jesus."

The man looked suspiciously at the boy for a moment, and then without a word turned on his heel and walked away.

And Dicky went on too, farther on, always to the East, but as near to the river as he could; for when the Star came out, he thought he would see it best there. But it got too dark at last, and he crept under an arch that looked on the river, and, as it was half boarded up, he found a nice corner out of the cold, biting wind, and was soon asleep. He was wakened, however, by something cold touching his face, and when he put out his hands to find what it was, he found a little thin cur of a dog, that shivered and licked his face, and cuddled in close beside him; tucking his jacket over it, he fell asleep again. But it wasn't very long before he was roused once more, and this time it was with a fright, as if a sack of rags had fallen on him, and when he wriggled about and cried out, the bundle got up—a half-tipsy woman! She dragged Dicky to the entrance of the arch, looked at him in the clear moonlight, and Dicky looked at her. She was a poor creature—a poor, sad creature.

"What are you doing here," she asked, "tripping up people like that?"

"I was just sleeping," he said; "I didn't know 'twere your house."

"Oh, didn't you?" she said, with a mocking laugh. "Didn't you see my name on the brass plate at the door? What are you after?"

"I'm after the Star," said Dicky, "the Star that leads to Jesus."

And then he told her all about it, as he had to the others.

"My boy," said the woman hoarsely, when he was done, "I can't make out all that you mean, but you are right about the Star. I went after it once myself, and then I had a good home, and a good husband and children, but I lost sight of the Star and took to drink, and I have lost everything since—everything;" and she flung herself down in the corner and would not speak more, though Dicky thought he heard her sobbing.

He could not sleep any more. A strong feeling came on him to run away, and he slipped out in the moonlight, and ran and ran, with the little cur yelping for joy round about him. On and on and on—on through the grey of the morning, on through the light of the noon, on to the gathering dark he trudged, with a strange feeling like fire within him, while all was frosty without, till he came where some fishing-smacks were drawn up on the beach. Against one of them was a ladder, and he went up, hardly knowing why— went up with the little cur in his arm, and down into the little cabin, and there lay on the floor, spent and weary, but with a strange burning feeling in his head, though he was shivering all over.

What a dream he had that night! He saw again the sailor man who had told him the way to the East, and saw bad angels gathering round him and drawing him away, till a Star shone out, and the man shook himself free. And he saw once more the young man he met at the river's brink, looking bright and glad as he spoke of the Star that had saved him from death. And he saw a bright fireside, with children, their faces ruddy in the firelight, and a broad-chested, manly-looking man, and a woman, the woman the children were gathered round, the same woman he had seen at the arch in the moonlight. "It was that word about the Star that did it," she said. And he saw the sky grow dark and dark, all but where a Star shone; but the Star grew brighter and brighter, and came nearer and nearer, and brighter and nearer still, till its light filled up everything, and right in the midst of the light there was One with a crown of gold on His head, with a kind, sweet face, a face that was somehow something like mother's, and He stooped and kissed the boy, and then he remembered no more.

In the morning some fishermen heard the dog barking on the boat, and when they tried to whistle it off or catch it, it always went back towards the cabin. And one went up and looked in, and saw Dicky there. They lifted him gently out, these rough, strong men with the fatherly hearts, and carried him to the little inn. A motherly soul was the inn-keeper's wife, and day and night she nursed the boy through his fever—ay, and with God's blessing she brought him round at last.

Dicky's a man now. He has been round the world again and again before the mast, but has come to anchor, as he says, on the East coast. Down there is the village of Crossford, where the shore is wild and rugged. When you go there next time, stroll down by the little house on the beach, where the lifeboat is kept, and you will see a notice stuck up, "For the key, apply to Richard Boy, Captain of the Lifeboat." That's what he is now—a brave, God-fearing man, who goes out with his crew in the wildest weather, when a ship has struck, and some lives may be saved. "It's the finest work in the world," he says, "this saving work; for as long as there is somebody you are trying to save, you are sure to be following the Star."

Yes, that is the story of Dicky Boy. If it can tell us anything, it can tell us this, that you can never follow the Star that leads to Jesus, you can never follow the truth and do what is right because you love the Lord and want to be His, but even when you are least aware of it, you are bound to be doing good. That Star that "went before them" left a long bright track in the sky, and your life and mine, and everybody's life, can do the same as we follow on, and still follow on, to know the Lord. All your days be sure of this: "There's a deal of good to be got by following the Star."

LIII

A NEW START

"One to be ready, two to be steady, three to be off, and—away!" That's the start, and we are getting it now. A new year, a new chance for a new life and a better one; toe the line!

Race fair. No tricks. Never "foul." Make up your mind that in all the coming year you will never "foul" your neighbour, never willingly get in his way so as to keep him back. Dodging is not running. If somebody else is doing better than you, give him room. Don't tell stories about him, or hurt his character, or hinder his work. The world is big enough for us all, and before the race is done some who were ahead will be behind, and more's the pity; but more will be the pity still if you have been the one to weaken him in the way. Race fair; a good conscience and a kind heart are better in the end than cups of gold.

Expect hindrances. Some you will have to meet from without—hard tasks, weary bits, rough places. *Rush* them. Most are only bogies; they disappear when you make a bold dash for them.

But your chief hindrances will come from yourself. You will get tired; people can become weary even in well-doing. The road will sometimes seem very uninteresting, and parts of it will be lonely. Then, though you mean well, as likely as not you won't run well, but you won't suspect it yourself. What you shall need then is some one to "give you the pace." Do you understand? When a runner is growing tired, he naturally slackens his rate; but if he is left to himself he may not find this out, for he can't go back and measure the rate he went at the first. So another runner, who is fresh, goes ahead of him, or runs by his side to keep him up to it.

Ah, children, children! it's a long run from New Year to New Year. Many shall faint and fail, and many who toed the line along with you shall have dropped from the running for ever before the winning-post is in sight. Do not take the pace, then, from any boy or girl, man or woman. There is but One who is always fresh, always faithful, always helpful—Jesus Christ. "Let us run with patience the race that is set before us, *looking unto Jesus.*" Take the pace from Him, start fair, keep Him ever before you, and you shall win. But only so.

There are many things you think you will need for a long race. Well, take them with you if you can, but do not carry more than you must. Leave to-morrow's troubles till to-morrow has come. A great many people tire themselves out by climbing hills before they reach them! It is enough just now to carry what Jesus gives you to carry *to-day*. Don't load up either with last year's failures. They were plentiful enough, I have no doubt, and sad enough too, but let the dead year bury its dead. What you have to do is to seek for life, and for life more and more abundantly, and you can't do that if you load up with old mistakes and failings. Ask the Lord to forgive all these, and then — leave them. Forget the things that are behind, and go *on* and go *up*. Lay in a stock of patience: that is the condensed extract of everything else you shall need. *Patience!* step over step, step over step—steady! It's dogged does it. And *hope!* always expect to find something good just round the next corner; expect sunshine after rain, and a smile after a frown. Patience and Hope: if these are in your kit, and you are looking unto Jesus, you will make for yourself what I wish for you all — a Happy New Year.

THE END

Printed by BALLANTYNE, HANSON & Co.
Edinburgh and London

www.ingramcontent.com/pod-product-compliance
Lightning Source LLC
Chambersburg PA
CBHW031352230426
43670CB00006B/518